TASTE AND TEMPERAMENT

TASTE
AND
TEMPERAMENT

A Brief Study of Psychological Types
in their Relation to the Visual Arts

by

JOAN EVANS, D.Litt., D.Lit.

Hon. Fellow of St. Hugh's College

JONATHAN CAPE
THIRTY BEDFORD SQUARE
LONDON

FIRST PUBLISHED 1939

JONATHAN CAPE LTD.   30 BEDFORD SQUARE, LONDON
AND 91 WELLINGTON STREET WEST, TORONTO

PRINTED IN GREAT BRITAIN IN THE CITY OF OXFORD
AT THE ALDEN PRESS
PAPER MADE BY JOHN DICKINSON & CO. LTD.
BOUND BY A. W. BAIN & CO. LTD.

CONTENTS

ILLUSTRATIONS

[All to be found at the end of the book]

ILLUSTRATIONS

ILLUSTRATIONS

PREFACE

WHEN in 1931 I published *Pattern*, I wrote in the Introduction:

> I think that a study of the conditions of creation in the decorative arts should precede a study of the psychology of beauty in arts of a more advanced and more personal kind.

I can hardly claim that the present brief study is of 'the psychology of beauty'; but it is an attempt to clear away certain generalizations, and to show that it is as important to discriminate between the types of perceiving men as it is to distinguish between the *genres* of art. There are two points which I wish to make clear. First, my work has no claims whatsoever to be a scientific investigation. Such an inquiry would only be possible could I collect some hundreds of people of artistic susceptibility and varying nationality and training, have the psychological temperament of each diagnosed by the same psychologist, and then escort them on a tour of the masterpieces of painting, architecture and sculpture, with facilities for recording the occasions when each one experienced the aesthetic thrill and his account of what caused it. I should be happy to offer myself as a subject for such an investigation, but am not prepared to undertake its organization.

Secondly, this is not a book of aesthetic philosophy. I have neither the training nor the temperament of a philosopher, and have no wish to trespass on his field. The book may, I hope, interest psychologists and students of aesthetics; but it is written with no more scientific exactitude, no more philosophic depth and no more ethical responsibility than any other piece of art criticism. If it has any value, it is firstly because it takes account of temperamental differences in the man who is spectator or artist; and secondly because it is concerned with the visual arts, that normally receive less consideration from the aesthetic thinker than the arts of music, drama and literature.

If I use an inordinate number of quotations, it is because the considered judgments of others, recorded with no thought of temperamental predilections, have necessarily a higher evidential value than anything I could say myself. Where no place of publication is given, a book written in English was published in London, one in French at Paris.

My thanks are due first and foremost to the friends who have helped in the making of this book by their encouragement, advice and criticism. Since they did not always agree with me, I do not name them; but my reason is discretion and not ingratitude. Next I must express my gratitude to the Keepers of Galleries and Museums, and to Mr. Joseph Widener, for allowing me to reproduce pictures from their collections.

J. E.

TASTE AND TEMPERAMENT

Il y a autant de beautés qu'il y a de
manières de chercher le bonheur.
                                    STENDHAL

CHAPTER I

THE THEORY OF THE
TEMPERAMENTS

Temperament ... is a very difficult subject which most
psychologists are glad to leave alone
W. McDougall, *An Introduction to Social
Psychology*, 21st ed. 1928, p. 99

A DISCUSSION of taste is necessarily linked with a conception of beauty. I am content to accept Aquinas'
definition: *id cujus ipsa apprehensio placet.*[1]   This definition
has lately been re-expressed by Professor Yrjö Hirn
in the form that 'beauty is the aesthetically effective'.
Such a definition may offend those who conceive of
visible beauty as the reflection or echo of an absolute
beauty; but in fact it is impossible to conceive of
beauty except in relation with a being who is moved by it.
Nor can the relation be one of pure emotion; intellect
enters into every artistic activity, whether of perception
or creation, for in every such activity judgment is exer-
cised, though it may be unconscious judgment. Therefore, if aesthetics be the study of the relation that exists
between the man who perceives beauty and the object
that he finds beautiful, it must include a study of that
combination of tendencies in feeling and bent in thought
which we call temperament. For this relation between
the perceiver and the thing perceived is subject to a

---

[1] *Summa* I. a 2 æ quaest. 27 art. 1. Hume expressed the idea more narrowly
in the famous dictum which inspired the aesthetic philosophy of Kant: 'Beauty
is no quality in things themselves; it exists merely in the mind which contemplates them.' The most recent application of Aquinas' doctrine will be found
in ERIC GILL, *Id quod visum placet*, 1926.

double variation: not only the works of art that are found beautiful, but also the men who perceive them, vary to a degree that disconcerts the philosopher. La Bruyère followed the thought of his time in admitting the existence only of Good and Bad Taste, but his honesty of mind drove him to admit that 'il y a beaucoup plus de vivacité que de goût parmi les hommes'.[1] Burke, again, who first predicated that 'it must necessarily be allowed, that the pleasures and the pains which every object excites in one man, it must raise in all mankind', had to continue: 'sensibility and judgment, which are the qualities that compose what we commonly call a *taste*, vary exceedingly in various people. From a defect in the former of these qualities arises a want of taste; a weakness in the latter constitutes a wrong or a bad one.'[2] When in the nineteenth century aesthetic theory became strongly influenced by physical science, Grant Allen[3] expressed the difficulty of arriving at scientific principles of aesthetics because of the variations of individual taste; but on the whole he considered taste to be fairly constant, if varying in degree. He talked of 'the highest' and 'the vulgarest', and did not attempt any more equal classification.

It would seem that before any valid generalizations on the nature of beauty can be made there must be much preliminary study of the thing perceived and the man who perceives it: the study of taste is a necessary pre-

[1] *Des ouvrages de l'Esprit.*
[2] *On the Sublime and Beautiful*: Introduction. Burke, however, was not concerned with works of visual art; his study of the sublime is related to literature and of the beautiful to physical beauty. The same view is also expressed by Richard Payne Knight in *An analytical enquiry into the Principles of Taste*, 1805, p. 1: 'As the organs of feeling and perception appear to be the same in the whole species, and only differing in degrees of sensibility, it should naturally follow that all would be pleased or displeased more or less, according to those different degrees of sensibility, with the same objects.'
[3] *Physiological Aesthetics*, 1877, p. 42.

liminary to the discovery of a theory of beauty. So far as the study of the thing perceived is concerned, we are fortunately situated. For more than two centuries men of learning and sensibility have been writing serious criticisms of visible works of art, and, in the century and a half since the French Revolution and the Napoleonic Wars heaped up the treasures of Europe into museums, the history of visual art has been scientifically studied.[1] In this time great progress has been made alike in the verbal expression of the emotional and intellectual sensations which a work of art inspires, and in the understanding of the historical circumstances which made its production possible.

More recently psychologists have begun to make progress in the study of the other necessity for aesthetic theory, the perceiving man. Yet the attempt to classify mankind into psychological types dates from the earliest years of science. Galen propounded the doctrine of the four temperaments, sanguine, phlegmatic, choleric and melancholic, corresponding with the four elements of Empedocles and the four organic fluids of Hippocrates. Plato, characteristically dissatisfied with a physical classification, attempted the creation of purely psychological categories.[2] He regarded the human soul as a complex whole consisting of three 'forms', 'kinds', 'or parts'. The first is ἐπιθυμία or appetite; and 'because wealth is the principal instrument by which the bodily appetites are satisfied, we call this element of the soul the wealth-loving or gain-loving element'. The second is θυμός, or spirit, that at its best is courage and at its worst

---

[1] The conception of a history of art is first found in WINCKELMANN in 1764, but he was concerned only with classical antiquity.

[2] *Republic*, Bk. III *et passim*; the whole admirably expounded in R. L. NETTLESHIP, The Theory of Education in Plato's *Republic* in *Hellenica*, ed. E. A. Abbot, 1898, p. 67 *et seq*.

pugnacity; it is the spiritual element that is capable of righteous indignation, and that which lies at the root of ambition. The third, and in Plato's view the highest, element in the human soul is 'the philosophic'. This element is a gentler counterpoise to θυμός, loving knowledge and taking a quiet pleasure in things and places and persons. It is also the calculating, deliberative, reasoning element in the soul, the element which when fully developed leads beyond the love of wisdom to Wisdom herself.

In the ninth book of the *Republic* Plato goes on to divide mankind into three 'primary kinds' according as one or other of the three psychical elements predominates: one category of men whose chief object in life is wealth; one category of those whose chief aim is honour; and one of those who above all else seek truth. The Gnostic philosophers inherited the tradition of three types from Plato, and classified them as the *Pneumatici* or thinkers, the *Psychici* or men of feeling, and the *Hylici* or materialists.[1] Such psychological classifications, however, did not form part of the Christian doctrine of the Middle Ages. Their influence was hardly felt until Hume[2] described with wit and skill 'The Epicurean, or the Man of Elegance and Pleasure'; 'The Stoic, or the Man of Action and Virtue'; 'The Platonist, or the Man of Contemplation and Philosophical Devotion'; and added 'The Sceptic', who seems to be a sub-species of the Gnostics' materialist.[3]

But if during the Middle Ages and the Renaissance Plato's classification was almost forgotten, the quaterni-

[1] See JUNG, *Psychological Types*, trans. Baynes, 1923, p. 18.
[2] *Essays, Moral, Political & Literary*, xv to xviii, 1875 ed., vol. I, p. 197.
[3] In more recent times Platonic influence is evident in Bain's three types: intellectual, emotional, volitional (*Study of Character*, 1861), and in M. DESSOIR'S *Seinsmensch, Lebensmensch and Leistungsmensch*. (See *Character and Personality*, III, 1935, p. 214.)

ties of Galen were perpetuated by medical science and astrology,[1] and passed from scientific thinking into the everyday philosophy of the common man. Even in the eighteenth century philosophers and doctors were content to accept them with little modification.[2] Thus Kant stressed the difference between the sanguine and melancholic temperaments, in which feeling preponderates, and the choleric and phlegmatic temperaments which are dominantly volitional.[3] To this criterion he added a secondary test, of the condition of tension or relaxation, and thus had criteria for establishing the four types. His contemporary Haller[4] made strength and irritability his tests for differentiation. Wundt made[5] strength and rapidity of motion his criteria; he classified the choleric as strong and quick; the melancholic as strong and slow, the sanguine as weak and quick, and the phlegmatic as weak and slow.[6]

[1] They were not accepted by the scholastic philosophers. See St. Thomas Aquinas, *Summa Philosophiæ*, lib. ii, cap. lxiii.

[2] Andreas Rüdiger in his *Physica divina* reduced the number of elements responsible for temperamental differences to a light element (aether) and a heavy (air), which might be refined or unrefined. Their combinations resulted in the familiar four temperaments. Stahl, who worked at Halle early in the eighteenth century, gave them a physical basis according to the thickness of the blood, the porosity of the tissues and the width of the blood vessels. On these and other modifications see A. A. Roback, *The Psychology of Character*, Cambridge, Mass., 1927, which also has an excellent bibliography.

[3] *Anthropologie*, Pt. II. See also Roback, op. cit., p. 51. Kant considered the sanguine light-blooded, the melancholic heavy-blooded, the choleric warm-blooded and the phlegmatic cold-blooded. His contemporary, Platner, made the predominance of visual, auditory and tactual nerves over the olfactory, gustatory and coenaesthetic nerves one criterion, and their strength and balance another. P. J. Cabanis makes a division according to the predominance of the muscular or nervous systems, 'des forces sensitives ou des forces motrices' (*Rapports du physique et du moral de l'homme*. 3 vols. Paris, 1824).

[4] In the *Elementa Physiologiae* cited by Roback, op. cit., p. 48. He substituted a 'sturdy peasant' for the sanguine type.

[5] And accepted Lotze's substitution of 'sentimental' for melancholic.

[6] See Wundt, *Principles of Physiological Psychology*, trans. Titchener, 1902, Pt. II. He rather ingenuously considered that a man can make use of all four temperaments at different times, and advised him to be sanguine in the minor joys and sorrows of everyday life, melancholic in more significant events, choleric in matters that claim his deepest interest and phlegmatic in the carrying out of resolutions. Wundt's main classifications were followed by B. Perez,

In the middle of the nineteenth century a tendency became evident to subdivide the classification of temperament. Fourier in 1849 so multiplied the potential varieties of character as to arrive at eight hundred and ten of them, on a system too complex to be summarized.[1] Such a scheme was chiefly of value in helping to free men's minds from the tyranny of the ancient quaternities. For a time there was a tendency to think that 'every sentiment tends to form a type of character of its own'.[2] Klages wished to reclassify mankind less by type than by 'a system of driving forces'.[3] Spranger devised a more fruitful scheme based on the determination of a dominant attitude of mind.[4] He distinguished four main attitudes: one that concentrated on economic significance and the measurement of energy; one that dwelt on the theoretic significance and essential being; one centred on aesthetic significance and imaginative beauty and one on religious significance and total meaning. Every mind, he considered, was capable of all these attitudes; but each mind was so biased that one attitude would always tend to be dominant, just as in a faulty set of dice one side would tend to fall uppermost at every throw.

Then the psychiatrists began to provide new scientific classifications. One of the most complete of these was

---

[1] C. FOURIER, *Passions of the Human Soul*, trans. R. J. Morell.
[2] A. F. SHAND, *The Foundations of Character*, 1920, p. 123. The tendency is exemplified in E. BOURDET, *Les Maladies du Caractère*, 1858, and F. PAULHAN, *Les Caractères*, 2nd ed. 1902.
[3] *The Science of Character*, trans. W. H. Johnston, 1929, p. 148.
[4] E. SPRANGER, *Types of Men*, trans. P. J. W. Pigors, Halle, 1928 (originally written 1914, rewritten 1920).

Le caractère de l'enfant à l'homme, 1891, A. FOUILLÉE, *Temperament et caractère*, 1896, J. RIBOT, *La Psychologie des Sentiments*, 1896, P. MALAPERT, *Les Elements du Caractere*, 1897, and by J. JASTROW, *Character and Temperament*, New York and London, 1915. F. JORDAN (*Character as seen in Body and Parentage*, 3rd ed. 1896, p. 5) made a predominant trend to action or to reflection his criteria; Southard the degree of energy. Ostwald also followed Wundt in making quickness and slowness of action his criteria. (See DOWNIE, *The Will Temperament*, 1923, p. 2.)

produced by Dr. Rosanoff in 1920.[1] He divided temperament into four main categories: the antisocial or hysteric type; the cyclothymic type, with four variants, manic, depressive, irascible and unstable; the autistic or shut-in type; and the epileptic type. His work was definitely concerned with morbid psychology, but he made some attempt to relate it to the normal mind. He was inclined to think that many temperaments were hybrid. Professor Dupré at almost the same moment[2] developed the idea of a permanent innate psychopathic constitution, which he classified as paranoiac, delinquent or perverse, mythomanic or hysteric, cyclothymic or hyperemotive. Dr. Kretschmer[3] followed him with six types: three cyclothyme — hypomanic, syntonic and phlegmatic; and three schizothyme — hyperaesthetic, moderate and anaesthetic.[4]

Jung, with his strong philosophic bent, broke away from such categories. His first contribution was a purely psychological classification into the now familiar categories of extravert and introvert. He defined the extravert as the man whose *libido*, or psychic energy, or interest, flows outwards to the object; for him objective facts or external happenings are the all-important factors of life. The attitude of the introvert is diametrically opposite. His interest is subjective; for him the significance of the object lies not in itself but in his own inter-

[1] 'A Theory of Personality, based mainly on Psychiatric Experience' in *Psychological Bulletin*, XVII, New York, 1920, p. 281.
[2] *Pathologie de l'imagination et de l'émotivité*, 1925, p. 485: this part of the book is based on an inaugural lecture given in 1919. Its doctrines were published in 1922 by F. ACHILLE-DELMAS and M. BOLL in *La personnalité humaine*.
[3] *A Text Book of Medical Psychology*, trans. E. B. Strauss, Oxford, 1934. He is interested in the parallel between somatic and temperamental types. See also his *Psychology of Men of Genius*, trans. R. B. Cattell, 1931, and *Physique and Character*, trans. W. J. H. Sprott, 1925.
[4] I am not qualified to summarize the more medical work of E. HURT (in *Grenzfr. des Nerven und Seelenlebens*, 1905, p. 62), MEUMANN, RORSCHACH and JAENSCH.

pretation of it. This broad classification of types he later modified to form a different and more complicated conception. Instead of types he defined an introvert and extravert attitude of mind in relation to the four mental functions of thought, feeling, intuition and sensation. The predominance of one of these functions, in his view, determines the type, while the extravert or introvert attitude may vary.[1]

According to Jung's classification, the man whose dominant function is logical thought,[2] if he be an extravert, bases the system of his life on logical conclusions arrived at through consideration of facts of objective experience or of generally accepted principles. When thought is the superior function of the introvert[3] it is subjective; it is concerned not with the intrinsic nature of the object but with his own idea of it. Such thought is not merely accumulative and constructive like that of the extravert, but is creative and theoretical.

The man whose dominant mental function is feeling, and his attitude of mind extraverted, is again objective.[4] His feeling is induced by the object itself or upon commonly accepted standards of valuation associated with it. If his attitude of mind be introverted, his feeling is subjective, critical, and based on his own valuation of it, which is often negative.

The sensation-type is again classified by Jung into extravert and introvert varieties.[5] The extravert finds reality in actual concrete objects, and the amount of sensation he derives from them sums up the value of living. The introverted sensation-type interposes his own subjective perception between himself and the object,

---

[1] For an account of his later views see R. G. GORDON, *Personality*, 1926; and JOAN CORRIE, *A.B.C. of Jung's Psychology*, 1927. The latter is particularly valuable as it is based on Jung's unpublished lectures.
[2] CORRIE, p. 38.   [3] Ibid., p. 39.   [4] Ibid., p. 41.   [5] Ibid., p. 44.

and thus puts into it something which does not belong to it but to his own view of it.

The intuitive type sees not what is but what may be. The extraverted intuitive is always on the look out for possibilities in the external situation; anything new fascinates him. His mind is constantly perceiving new combinations and alterations of existing reality in accordance with the possibilities he sees ahead. The introverted intuitive is not concerned with external facts. His perception is subjective, focused upon the images he finds in the unconscious. His sight is turned within and there amid the wealth of archetypes he finds the material necessary for his vision.[1]

The most recent writer on human temperament, Dr. Murdo Mackenzie, again reaffirms the doctrine of an innate and consistent type of temperament. His classification[2] is based on two criteria: the speed of reaction and the acceptance of amplification or simplification as a standard of value. The distinction between these two qualities of thinking — concrete or discrete, amplifying or simplifying — is definitely laid down; and the theory of an innate and consistent type of temperament strongly upheld.

It will be seen that the very conception of an innate permanent temperament, though thus recently and strongly reaffirmed, is not at the moment axiomatic in psychology. Yet I venture, as a layman, to think that the conception of temperament as 'an aggregate of tendencies

[1] CORRIE, p. 44.
[2] See *When Temperaments Clash, a study of the components of human Temperament*, 1937. In this work he classifies temperaments as exemplified by the craftsman, whose pace is deliberate and whose sense of value is simplification; the advertiser, whose pace is immediate and whose sense of value is simplification; the dealer, whose pace is immediate, and whose sense of value is amplification; and the administrator, whose pace is deliberate, and whose sense of value is amplification.

expressing the general deportment of the organism, the manner in which it functions, the tone, value, and direction of its vitality'[1] is not the least precious doctrine of our ancient philosophic inheritance. But I would use the doctrine as befits its ancestry, less scientifically than humanistically. The inherent variations of human character are not congenial matter for statistics nor fit material for a graph; nor can they most fruitfully be studied in their simplest and crudest forms, but rather in their most accomplished and most mature.

This is most clearly evident, I think, in the domain of human taste. Much research has been done into individual preferences for simple forms and colours, lines and balance,[2] but little into preferences for works of art. Even when this is attempted the human material available for experiment is too often immature[3] and the 'artistic' material deplorable.[4]

Dr. Bullough in his experiments on colour perception found four types of perception: an objective type that

[1] FOUILLÉE, *Tempérament et Caractère*, 1895, p. 358.

[2] See E. BULLOUGH, 'The "Perceptive-Problem" in the aesthetic appreciation of colours', in *British Journal of Psychology*, II, 1906-8, Cambridge, 1908, p. 418; 'The "Perceptive-Problem" in the aesthetic appreciation of simple colour combinations', ibid. III, 1909-10, p. 406; 'Recent Work in Psychological Aesthetics', ibid. XII, 1921-2, p. 81. C. W. VALENTINE, *An Introduction to the Experimental Psychology of Beauty*, 2nd ed. 1919; H. S. ZANGFELD, *The Aesthetic Attitude*, New York, 1920; E. D. PUFFER, 'Studies in Symmetry' in *Psychological Review*, Harvard Psychological Studies, vol. I, Monograph Supplements, IV, New York, 1903, *The Psychology of Beauty*, Cambridge, Mass, 1905, especially pp. 94 and 128 *et seq.*; Dr. KATZ, *The World of Colour*, 1935.

[3] This point is well brought out in M. W. CALKINS, 'An attempted Experiment in Psychological Aesthetics' in *Psychological Review*, VII, New York, 1900, p. 580.

[4] Exception should be made for certain musical studies. *Comment faut-il écouter la Musique?* by C. ODIER, quoted by C. BAUDOIN, *Psychanalyse de l'Art*, p. 192, gives five categories: the rational technicians, the 'idéatifs' who seek in music the expression of abstract ideas, the imaginatives who see a succession of visual images, the sentimentalists, who find in any piece of music the expression of some particular shade of emotion, and the pure emotionalists, who enjoy without any attempt at identifying the quality of their enjoyment. Similar inquiries, with somewhat similar results, have also been made by Seashore and Delacroix.

found colours washy, unusual, good, and so on; a physiological type, that found them cheering, depressing, cold,
warm, and so on; a type that attributed to them human
characteristics — insipidity, friendliness, gloominess, deli-
cacy, and so forth; and a fourth type of which the perception was tinged by associations of every kind. Such a
piece of research is an honest step in the right direction,
but it is a long way from simple colours to works of art.
A more important distinction was made by Dessoir,[1] who
noted the difference between those who first saw formal
features and those who first perceived the content of a
picture. His distinction, arrived at by experimental research, was also arrived at empirically by critics of art,
who were dealing not with the spectator but with the
artist himself. Roger Fry recognized two groups of
artists, one 'mainly preoccupied with creating a fantasy-
world in which the fulfilment of wishes is realized',[2] the
other 'concerned with the contemplation of formal relations'.[3] T. E. Hulme[4] defined two kinds of art, geometrical and vital, each springing from 'a certain general
attitude towards the world'. According to him the vital,
or naturalistic, type of art — exemplified by that of
Greece and Rome — exists to satisfy an empathy-wish;[5]
the geometric, typified by Byzantine mosaics and Epstein's sculptures, to satisfy a tendency to abstraction.
Naturalistic art is the result of a happy pantheistic relation between man and the outside world, abstract art
the result of a feeling of separation in face of external

---

[1] 'Das Beschreiben von Bildern' in *Zeitschrift für Aesthetik*, VIII, p. 440.
[2] This seems to correspond with Professor Wilenski's 'original romantic art'.
All the artists he cites — Botticelli, Rossetti, Rembrandt, Delacroix, Van Gogh,
Daumier, Guys, Rodin, Degas, Epstein and John – I should classify as extravert (*Modern Movement in Art*, 1935, p. 71).
[3] *The Artist and Psycho-Analysis* (The Hogarth Essays), 1924, p. 3.
[4] *Speculations*, 1924, p. 77.
[5] See p. 59.

nature. Professor Collingwood[1] in his turn defines two categories. 'One type waits on the subject. The subject must come to him and excite him, inspire him, raise his artistic faculties above the pitch of mediocrity, which is all he can achieve when the subject is less exciting to him. The other type takes the initiative. He does not wait for the subject to arouse his faculties; he is a skilled man, the master of a craft, and he chooses a subject for the exhibition of his skill with no more emotion than that with which the surgeon contemplates the case on which he is about to operate.'

Even such categories — corresponding roughly to the ideas of classical and romantic, extravert and introvert — have had little influence on the modern aesthetic applications of psychological thought. For the pioneers of modern psychology are little concerned with beauty. Freud[2] dismisses the love of beauty as 'a perfect example of a feeling with an inhibited aim'; Jung's chapter on aesthetics is extraordinarily confused and largely devoted to quotation.[3] Most aesthetic thinkers seem still to be willing to base their theories on an Abstract Man: the same Abstract Man who has been a stumbling-block to generations of economic thinkers. Unfortunately, some two-thirds of the human race are apt to behave differently from the Abstract Man, and in no sphere more markedly than in their reaction to works of art.

[1] 'Form and Content in Art' in *Journal of Philosophical Studies*, IV, 1929, p. 334.

[2] *Civilisation and its Discontents*, 1930, p. 39. He repeats the view that art lies outside psycho-analysis in his study of Leonardo da Vinci, see also Le Moïse de Michelange, in *Rev. francaise de psychanalyse*, I, 1927, p. 120; E. JONES, *Essays in applied Psycho-analysis*, 1923, p. 265; and C. BAUDOUIN, *Psychanalyse de l'Art*, 1929, p. 55. A criticism of the Freudian view will be found in A. M. BODKIN, 'The Relevance of Psycho-Analysis to Art Criticism' in *British Journal of Psychology*, XV, 1924-5, Cambridge 1925, p. 174, and C. MAURON, *Aesthetics and Psychology*, trans. R. Fry and K. John, 1935.

[3] *Psychological Types*, chapter vii, The problem of typical attitudes in aesthetics.

My thesis is that generalizations on the relation between the perceiving and the perceived cannot profitably be made without further study and classification of the perceiving man. In this book, since I am no philosopher, I do not attempt to achieve any such aesthetic generalization, but I strive to interpret the most recent serious classification of human temperaments in terms of the visual arts,[1] in the hope that such studies, pushed further by others, may perhaps lead to a theory of art that will prove fruitful in its application.

[1] I exclude from this brief study a consideration of the art of primitive peoples, who sought not beauty but religious associations, magical power, or a mimetic assurance of strength. On the psychological implications of primitive art I would refer the reader to Yrjö Hirn, *The Origins of Art*, 1900; COMTE BÉGOUEN, 'The Magical Origins of Prehistoric Art' in *Antiquity*, 1929, III, p. 5; and BALDWIN BROWN, *The Art of the Cave-Dweller*, 1928.

CHAPTER II

PSYCHOLOGICAL TYPES

So then the first article of this knowledge is to set down
sound and true distributions, and descriptions of the
several characters and tempers of men's natures and disposi-
tions

BACON, *Advancement of Learning*, VII, 3

IF psychological types exist, as I believe they do, they
can be studied and described from such different aspects
that a series of parallel rather than similar descriptions
will be achieved. The alienist who looks upon their
pathological manifestations, the psychiatrist who is concerned with their therapeutic implications, the psychologist interested in the scientific study of the functions of
the mind, will all seize upon different aspects of the truth;
and the student of taste, as he approaches the same
problem from yet another angle, will describe human
propensities from the standpoint of his own preoccupation. Such a student is not immediately concerned with
the relation of one temperament to another; his interest
is focused on each type considered as a self-contained
entity, with an innate bias in taste as in all else. Therefore I have described the psychological types from my
own angle and in my own terms. I use extravert and
introvert as Jung originally defined them:[1] the extravert
as the man for whom objective facts and external happenings are the all important factors in life, and the
introvert as the man for whom the significance of the
object lies not in itself but in his own interpretation of it.

[1] See page 23.

I subdivide these categories according to the pace of their reaction, and so arrive at a classical quaternity of temperaments.

Many people will say that they have no expressible reaction to works of art, but in fact every person who is free to modify his environment by choosing or changing the furnishings of his room not only expresses his taste in art but also in some degree achieves artistic creation. I will, therefore, consider first this universal if wordless attitude to art; then the more conscious attitude to works of art formally regarded as such; and, finally, the profounder aesthetic emotion felt by those who are professedly artists.

The first type to be considered is the man whose reaction is slow, and his natural habit of mind impersonal, amplifying and concrete.[1] This slow extravert is characterized by the capacity for deliberate perseverance and organization. Material power is his ambition. It is in his stars to become the dictator, the soldier, the organizer and head of any and every institution; the art of politics and the code of laws are his predestined tools.[2] By nature he has little care and less respect for the feelings and thoughts of other individuals, and thus achieves independence if not isolation; but this detachment is counterpoised by a distrust of others who have different speeds

---

[1] See also MURDO MACKENZIE, *When Temperaments Clash*, chapter x.

[2] Cf. Jung's extravert thinker: 'He readily finds a role to fit him as natural scientist, politician, financier, advocate, ecclesiastic, architect, engineer, or any line where constructive ability of an objective kind is required. Owing to the inflexibility of his intellectual judgments, when the type is extreme he is apt to be intolerant, fanatical, even tyrannical; as for example a Torquemada; or, on a smaller scale, the domestic tyrant; there irrational perceptions are permitted no place in his scheme of things; but as life is never regulated by logic alone, these find a place in the unconscious. Here life in accordance with logical conclusions is arrived at through consideration of facts of objective experience or of generally accepted principles. He accumulates facts, for which he has the greatest possible respect.' CORRIE, op. cit., p. 28. The type roughly corresponds with Spranger's man whose dominant attitude of mind is concentrated on economic significance and the measurement of energy. See p. 22.

of thought and different scales of value from himself. He generally has a contempt for 'the foreigner', but enjoys travel in the desert places of the earth. He is at times weighed down by a consciousness of the complexity of material facts, from which his mind permits no logical escape. He may lighten this burden by belief in a God who has created and will protect him; but this God he makes in his own image, a jealous God who avenges the breaking of taboos and the neglect of ritual. His religion is neither mystical, humanitarian nor philosophical, but dogmatic. Alternatively, he may find escape in the search after an Absolute, that exists in some other world of thought than the manifold, incomplete and uncomprehended world of fact. 'A défaut d'une victoire effective sur le monde, l'on se contentera de la victoire apparente que semblent assurer les religions et les métaphysiques. Nous sentons qu'il est définitivement interdit aux hommes de vaincre réellement la mort, d'abolir réellement le temps, de dominer réellement tout ce qui nous limite et nous exclut. Mais qu'importe cela, si nous réussissons à nous persuader que nous tenons le moyen d'accéder à une réalité qui dépasse infiniment l'univers?'[1]

The *forte* of the slow extravert thinker is facts, and the methodical arrangement of facts. The academic type of scholarship is his stronghold. He does not interpret facts, but collects them; much as he does not make money constructively, but saves it. Normally he sticks to facts; but he is often credulous when he wishes to believe, and may for motives of his own advancement claim inspiration or revelation. When he does so it is always a confession of weakness. He tends to cultivate the society of his superiors or his inferiors rather than of his equals, for

[1] L. VIALLE, *Le désir du néant, contribution à la psychologie du divertissement.* Paris, 1933, p. 29.

32

with his equals an innate tendency to jealousy forbids the needed sense of trust. The clash of drama makes a peculiar appeal to his consciousness of power and domination. When he turns to writing, the cognate *genres* of epic and biography are his natural spheres of literary art.[1] Music he best loves combined with drama; Wagnerian opera must have been created for his especial delectation. His philosophy is an Aristotelian philosophy of division. Mentally inelastic, physically courageous, and practically capable, half the world regards him with admiration and half with hatred. If he lose his mental balance, he will tend to fall a victim to one of the forms of paranoia[2]: megalomania, miserliness, persecution mania or some expression of a sadistic tendency.

The slow extravert has usually little or nothing in his room that is not either practical or associated with his history. By an instinct (that when it is perverted will lead to the indiscriminate hoarding of worn-out possessions) he surrounds himself with mementoes of himself and his family; portraits, plate, souvenirs of his schools and colleges, his travels and wars, the men he has met and the ancestors he is proud of. A slow extravert will keep in view the water colours his aunt painted, and the cupboard made from the pews of his grandfather's church; he is likely to collect pictures of places where his family has lived. His rooms never have any decorative scheme and may seem superficially a mass of incongruities, but almost every object in them will be found to have a personal link with the owner. The one thing which may pull them together from the decorative point of view is a liking for plain massive surfaces. A moulding or a cornice repels the slow extravert as much as it

[1] Cf. HAVELOCK ELLIS, *A Study of British Genius*, 1927, p. 224. He considers that the nordic spirit recounts 'storm-swept days' in 'great architectonic poems' and cites the 'Chanson de Roland' as a type.   [2] See Dupré, op. cit. p. 485

attracts a quick introvert; he has what Ruskin calls 'our English way of liking nothing and professing to like triglyphs'.[1] His present ideal is a modernistic flat without an unnecessary ornament in it; but if that lie beyond his means he can be very happy with 1860 mahogany.

This comparative simplicity of furniture is redressed in other ways. His walls are generally laden with pictures and he has cabinets full of odds and ends, each with its associations.[2] He is the man who collects things either for their associations or for their possible rise in value. He buys with a sort of scholarship things not necessarily beautiful but with a lore of their own: stamps, old china, engravings in various states, letters and first editions. He is one of 'these inferior Virtuosi' who, 'in seeking so earnestly for Raritys, fall in love with Rarity for Rareness-sake'.[3] You will recognize him as he draws a bunch of keys from his trouser pocket and locks the case.

The next type of man — I keep the word, though the *fine fleur* of the type is generally recognized as feminine — has the same concrete and extraverted point of view, but his pace is not deliberate but immediate.[4] Consequently, though his relation to others does not involve great emotional intensity, it does involve considerable psychological dexterity. He does not, like the slow extravert, ignore the feelings of others; he is often skilful in understanding them, and sometimes in using them to his own advantage. He is the actor, the salesman, the courtier; she is — according to her degree — the social success, the 'grande amoureuse' or the harlot; they attain

---

[1] *Modern Painters*, I, 1843, chapter ii, p. 13.
[2] A person of this type who is not fully developed will have the same accumulation, but on another scale; his passion is for things minute and thus childish. Toy ornaments of every kind will be his pleasure and 'Titania's Palace' must have been made for his especial delectation.
[3] ANTHONY EARL OF SHAFTESBURY, *Characteristicks*, 1723, III, p. 157.
[4] See also MACKENZIE, op. cit., chapter ix.

success not by imposing their personality by force, but by 'getting it across'. Their goal of social success and the means they pursue to attain it may lead them into insincerity and self-indulgence. Their aim is pleasure and material enjoyment, and they excel in devising, enjoying and sharing this pleasure in Society. 'L'art de se faire valoir' is their prerogative, and very gracefully can they exercise it. Their interest even in learning is not always disinterested: with them it is apt to become a social art. Ultimately their universe is ego-centric. Yet, perhaps because their human ambition is as great as that of the slow extravert, but can find a less lasting satisfaction in material power, it is the quick extravert type that produces the great mystics. M. Vialle[1] defines thus their essential problem: 'Ils ont compris, senti, vécu jusqu'à l'angoisse, la détresse de n'être pas Dieu.' The only escape is to achieve direct communion with the God who is greater than themselves, in visions and trances and ecstasies, that exalt not only their God but also themselves to whom He is thus made manifest.[2] Thus many quick extraverts, living on a less lofty plane than St. Theresa or St. John of the Cross, are none the less able, if circumstances or their own free will deprive them of the usual satisfactions of life, to turn their emotions into impersonal channels and to tread the 'mystic way' of impersonal love. Their characteristic philosophy is one of illumination, a matter rather of *yoga* than of logical thinking. Since their universe is ego-centric they either tend, like Blake, to create a language of their own, or else, like many mystics, to use ordinary language esoterically. They are the visionary romantics who appreciate what is glamorous and sentimental; their natural trend

[1] Op. cit., p. 6.
[2] This aspect of the type has something in common with Spranger's type, whose mind is predominantly concentrated on religious meaning. See p. 22.

in poetry is to the pure lyric. If they lose their mental balance, they become hysteric.[1]

Both quick and slow extraverts think of their surroundings as a background; but if for one it is an autobiography, for the other it is a *mise-en-scène*. For the quick extravert, art is significant in so far as it can be turned to enhance his attractiveness. For this reason a quick extravert's room is generally a place of soft colours, elegant draperies, and well-shaded lights; a few touches of gilding accent the whole. Colour is stressed more than form, but is generally subdued, and often faded and shaded. The quick extravert believes with Oscar Wilde that 'all beautiful colours are graduated colours, the colours that seem about to pass into one another's realm';[2] and delights, as Vernon Blake declares the Celtic imagination does, in 'the graceful but imperfect suggestion of a glasslike transparency and frail elegance'.[3] There is sometimes a certain want of courage in the scheme, but there is definitely a scheme; there is little sense of historical congruity but a real feeling for effectiveness. The fundamental defect is a sense of fashion so strong that unless the scheme is soon changed it becomes outmoded. It is the quick extravert's histrionic sense that creates the rooms that can be successfully photographed for reproduction.

If these are the extraverts, the introverts are their opposites. For them the interpretation is as important as the fact, and their relation with others as important as their conception of themselves. Jung[4] has defined their standpoint as one 'that under all circumstances sets the self and the subjective psychological process above the object and the objective process'. Yet although their

---

[1] See Dupré, loc. cit.
[2] O. WILDE, *Art and Decoration, being Extracts from Reviews & Miscellanies,* 1920, p. 20.
[3] *Relation in Art,* p. 130.   [4] *Psychological Types,* p. 12.

attitude is thus social and personal, their way of thinking is not concrete, but in the metaphysical sense of the word discrete. They do not amplify knowledge into a *corpus*, but simplify it into a theory.[1] The introvert with an immediate reaction[2] is vividly conscious of visible things, but sees them less from the concrete point of view than as material for interpretation. To discover cause and effect in direct action is his intellectual pleasure, and to enjoy argumentative converse with his equals his social ambition. Hogarth, defining his Abstract Perceiving Man,[3] describes a typical quick introvert: 'The active mind is ever bent to be employ'd. Pursuing is the business of our lives; and even abstracted from any other view, gives pleasure. Every arising difficulty that for a while attends or interrupts the pursuit, gives a sort of spring to the mind, enhances the pleasure, and makes what would else be toil and labour become sport and recreation.' William Morris was of this temperament[4] and in his description of what he considered the workman's due unconsciously sketches the life that a man of this sort hopes to lead. For him the Rights of Man were: 'Money enough to keep him from want or degradation for him and his; leisure enough from bread-earning work (even though it be pleasant to him) to give him time to read and think, and connect his own life with the life of the great world; work enough of the kind aforesaid, and praise of it, and encouragement enough to make him feel good friends with

[1] In many aspects this type corresponds with the introverted thinker-type of Jung. See CORRIE, p. 39. G. SÉAILLES (who appears to identify genius with this temperament) writes: 'Une même loi dirige toutes ses démarches, une même tendance est présente à tous ses actes: la multiplicité des idées le disperserait; par cela même qu'il vit, il les ordonne . . .' *Essai sur le Génie dans l' Art*, 1883, p. 3.
[2] Cf. MACKENZIE, op. cit., chapter viii.
[3] *Analysis of Beauty*, London, 1753, p. 24. There is some doubt whether Hogarth did indeed write the whole book.
[4] He suffered when overstrained from the alternation of elation and depression characteristic of this temperament. MACKAIL, *Life of William Morris*, I, p. 137.

his fellows; and lastly . . . . his own due share of art, the chief part of which will be a dwelling that does not lack the beauty which nature would freely allow it, if our perversity did not turn nature out of doors . . . No work which cannot be done with pleasure in the doing is worth doing.'[1] The quick introvert will forgive anything but boredom. He is the enthusiast who creates and reforms without counting the cost; 'all or nothing' is his motto. His imagination is vivid enough to see what must be done and how to do it; but he is often too impatient, too intolerant, too apt to think that everyone must see with his particular vision, to achieve success. His 'unruly affections' are exactly those stigmatized by Richard Hooker: 'self-love, vainglory, impatience, pride, pertinancy; these be the bane of our peace'. He may be a public benefactor or he may be a public nuisance, but his bent is always active. He is the intellectual romantic, sensitive to the romance of history, whether in its broad outlines or in the details of social life, to the charm of distance whether in time or space.[2] So Hazlitt described Charles Lamb, 'tenacious of the obscure and remote'. If the slow extravert is by nature a writer of biography, the quick introvert is the born autobiographer. Jean de Joinville, the earliest survivor in the *genre*, stands as example: his vanity and self-assertion, his loyalty and simplicity, his ready speech and his vivid visual memory, all declare him to be of this type. The mind of the quick introvert is apt to have a polymathic quality, the antithesis of the limited and exact scholarship of the slow extravert. He enjoys the stimulus of travel in known lands, of

---

[1] MACKAIL, *Life of William Morris*, II, p. 63.
[2] Cf. HAVELOCK ELLIS, *A Study of British Genius*, 1927, p. 217: 'In Celtic literature always there is present to us the *remote as remote* . . . not attained by the use of any cheap devices of mistiness and vagueness, but clearly and firmly by the hand of a great artist.'

which the beauty is enhanced by the works of man and the romance heightened by memories of history. His natural bent in poetry is to the intellectualized lyric, whether ode or sonnet. He is not burdened but stimulated by the actual world; he finds it, as William Morris did, 'beautiful and strange and dreadful and worshipful'[1], and does not, like the extravert, seek escape from it in the search for an Absolute or in the pursuit of a mystic religion. His intellectual bent is towards the study of immediate cause and effect.[2] For this reason he is not truly philosophical, since ultimate causes interest him little. His is rather the naturalism of the medieval school of Chartres, that found in the material world the image of the eternal ideas; or the humanism of Goethe, of a man who 'feels himself one with nature, and consequently looks upon the outside world not as something strange, but as something which he recognises as answering to his own feelings'. His religion is nearly always a cause to be preached and practised for human betterment; he may be a crusader or a revivalist, or he may be a humanitarian agnostic.

If the quick introvert's activity pass into aggression, or if it be frustrated and repressed overmuch, he may become the manic inmate of an asylum.

The quick introvert's interest in art is more impersonal, in the sense that he is unconscious of it as a background to himself, and more emotional, in that every object he sees is valued according to the aesthetic emotion it

---

[1] MACKAIL, *Life of William Morris*, I, p. 328.
[2] Cf. CLUTTON-BROCK's study of Leonardo da Vinci (*Essays on Art*, 1919, p. 18): 'To Leonardo causation meant the escape from caprice; it meant a secure relation between man and all things, in which man would gain power by knowledge, in which every increase of knowledge would reveal to him more and more of the supreme reason. There was no chain for him in cause and effect, no unthinking of the will of man . . . He knew that . . . you can learn nothing from reality unless you adore it, and in adoring it he found his freedom.'

inspires. The quick introvert is genuinely capable of an aesthetic emotion that is disinterested and profound, and for him the quest of aesthetic emotion may take the place of the quest of religious emotion and become a spiritual 'way of life'.[1] The quick introvert's room will often be over-full and generally be untidy, but everything in it, if he has means enough, will be there because it gives him aesthetic pleasure. He usually enjoys rich, deep, and glowing colours, and will put them together with a cheerful optimism that often achieves its effect. Plain colour pleases him less than colour wrought into a decorative pattern, but he demands more than colour.[2] Form matters to him: his furniture will probably be more shapely than padded, and the lines of his room and his furniture will be set off with cornices and mouldings. He is peculiarly sensitive to what Hogarth[3] calls 'the beauty of a composed intricacy of form'. For him, as Hogarth writes,[4] since pursuing is the aim of the active mind, 'Simplicity without variety is wholly insipid, and at best does only not displease . . . Intricacy of form . . . *leads the eye a wanton kind of chace*, and from the pleasure that gives the mind, intitles it to the name of beautiful'.

On the other hand, the quick introvert will probably not have many pictures,[5] and what there are will be thought of as part of the decoration of the whole room rather than as detached objects in it. That Renaissance invention, the 'easel-picture', is anathema to the quick

[1] Cf. Spranger's type predominantly concerned with aesthetic significance and imaginative beauty. See p. 22.

[2] Cf. CLIVE BELL, *Art*, p. 236: 'Colour becomes significant only when it becomes form.'

[3] *Analysis of Beauty*, p. 28.

[4] Ibid., pp. 21 and 24.

[5] William Morris was a typical quick introvert, and his biography records that 'his house was, with few exceptions for which there were special reasons, pictureless, and he never bought a picture after the early days when he had ceased trying to paint them.' MACKAIL, II, p. 274.

introvert; he would always prefer to have his pictures built into the panelling.

The quick introvert normally collects things because they seem to him beautiful, but his delight in tracing cause and effect may also lead him to collect what is less beautiful than interesting. A 'type-series' will always attract him, and so if he has one object of a kind he will be tempted to multiply it in order to study the development of the type. His motto might be that used by the collector Sauvageot, 'Dispersa coegi'. Thus any one of his possessions may become the basis of a collection: a collection probably ill-kept[1] but logical and alive.

The man of the fourth type is as personal in his bent, more simplifying and more discrete in his thinking, and more deliberate in his pace.[2] The slow introvert is less impelled to get things done, but more driven to understand their ultimate philosophical causes. His fellow-men are his natural preoccupation; he does not wish to dominate them, to impress them, or to influence their actions, but to understand them. Unlike the quick introvert, he does not found his thoughts upon an empirical (and sometimes opportunist) basis; his is the self-contemplating reason of the true philosopher. When Hugh of St. Victor described the scholarly life, progressing from *cogitatio* through *meditatio* to *contemplatio*, as 'the search for wisdom in quietude',[3] he wrote as a slow introvert. Plato is the predestined master of such thinkers. If the slow introvert's work lies with material things, he will love and respect the inherent qualities of his material; and if among humans, he will have the same respect for their

[1] The quick introvert tends to dislike the Museum atmosphere which appeal to the slow extravert's institutional tastes.
[2] Cf. MACKENZIE, op. cit., chapter vii. The type has much in common with Spranger's type of the man predominantly concerned with theoretic significance and essential being. See p. 22.
[3] A. E. TAYLOR, *The Mediaeval Mind*, II, p. 355.

natural qualities. His typical failing is that *défaitisme* which the medieval Church called *accidie*. The slow introvert has a natural bent towards true Christianity, but his religion is ill-defined and pervasive; there is more of Faith and Charity in it than of Hope, and nothing of the organized Church. It is, indeed, not a religion in the dogmatic sense, but a philosophy to guide the individual on his pilgrimage through life.

The written word that he can ponder at leisure means much to the slow introvert; he may even be tempted to define all art in its terms, and to say, with Professor Collingwood: 'Art must be language'.[1] Unless he approach them as a practising artist, the 'appearances' of the world of visible art often inspire him with a certain distrust. Institutions and committees are anathema to him as means to action, and only interesting since they show human minds in a complex relation. His ideal world is *à deux*, with all his interest focused on his companion. If the existing world prove too much for him, he falls into melancholia.

The slow introvert is the man whose artistic tastes lie farthest from expression. He has not the facile response of the introvert or extravert with a quick reaction, nor the slow extravert's capacity for confusing aesthetic emotion with extraneous but more congenial matter. It is true to say that in the visible world of art there is comparatively little that affords him positive pleasure.[2] When it comes to furnishing his room he is apt to let someone else do it for him; he will always be at the mercy of an incongruous or ugly gift. If the observer is

[1] *Principles of Art*, Oxford, 1938, p. 273.
[2] In Jung's introverted feeling-types 'feeling is subjective, critical, and often apparently depreciative of the object, since it does not depend primarily on the object itself but on the individual's own valuation of it, which is frequently negative.' CORRIE, p. 41.

fortunate enough to find a room a slow introvert has furnished himself he will recognize it as characteristic. There is an almost total absence of contrasted colour; the transition from cream to brown or from grey to blue is enough.[1] The patterns are few and simple, and often confined to those that arise out of the exigencies of ceramic or textile processes. There is hardly anything that is not for use, but everything is well proportioned, simple and well shaped. The pictures are very few and are likely to be engravings. It is neither a *mise-en-scène* nor an art gallery nor an illustrated biography but a workroom. If the owner be a woman, and her work that of making her family happy, it will have a peculiar intimate charm of its own, infinitely removed from the social brilliance of the quick extravert's *salon*, or from the individualist idiom of the quick introvert's abode.

These four types, thus linked and divided by the speed and quality of their reactions, cover the mature human species. I have described them in their fundamentals. It goes without saying that a highly civilized individual, not under any stress or strain, may not at once reveal his inmost characteristics; it goes without saying, too, that an individual of strong character, if he be aware of the defects of his temperament, may consciously overcome them. The self-indulgent man of quick extravert type may, like Saint Francis, find freedom at the hands of the Lady Poverty; the jealous slow extravert peace in the

---

[1] Professor J. A. Stewart has remarked on the comparative absence of colour-sense in Plato. *The Myths of Plato*, 1905, p. 381. Wordsworth was a typical slow introvert, and Havelock Ellis has noted his especial (and characteristic) predilection for green and grey in his poems, and the fact that he was not keenly sensitive to the joy of strong colour (*The Colour Sense in Literature*, 1931, p. 18). *A Plea for Art in the Home*, anonymously published *c.*1879, recommends a slow introvert scheme of decoration that seems to touch on caricature: grey paper for the drawing-room, with inscriptions from the Book of Job such as 'Man is born unto travail as the sparks fly upward' painted on it in black letters in diagonal lines.

43

bosom of the Benedictine Order. The quick introvert may discipline his mind in work of minute accuracy, and the slow introvert in the routine of practical life. But, manifest or not, such are the types of humanity. Their inter-relation is life; the amelioration of that inter-relation is the task of the psychiatrist. I venture to think that the investigation of their reactions to art is a necessary preliminary to any theory of aesthetics.

CHAPTER III

TASTE IN THE FINE ARTS

It is not we who judge a work of art; rather it is the work
of art that judges us

JOHN LA FARGE

WHEN it comes to the appreciation of works of art of a sort that lie outside schemes of house decoration, the quick extravert unconsciously demands a dream-inducing quality. For him, as for Monsieur Bergson, 'L'objet de l'art est d'endormir les puissances actives ou plutôt résistantes de notre personnalité, et de nous amener ainsi à un état de docilité parfaite où nous réalisons l'idée qu'on nous suggère, où nous sympathisons avec le sentiment'.[1] For him, to quote Lange,[2] 'that aesthetic enjoyment which a work of art as work of art affords is dependent neither upon the quality of its content nor upon its formal nature, but . . . rests entirely upon the strength and vividness of the illusion to which the artist brings us through his art'. These dreams and illusions may be amorous, and may lead to what Mr. Clutton Brock calls 'harem art',[3] with which we are all familiar; or they may lead to a mystic art that represents the nobler visions of the emotional nature of the quick extravert. Such art tends to have a hypnotic and trance-

[1] *Données immédiates de la conscience*, p. 11.
[2] K. LANGE, *Das Wesender Kunst*, p. 81.
[3] He says that out of the art of the Court of Louis XV 'there has sprung a harem art of the whole world which has infested the homes even of perfectly respectable ladies ever since'. *Essays on Art*, p. 27.

45

inducing quality[1] (to put it into an extreme form) that depends upon effects of glitter and light. The artistic standpoint of such mystics was expressed in the philosophy of the School of Plotinus, that made ecstasy rather than reason the organ of apprehension. Not only was a mystical union claimed between seer and seen,[2] but beauty was itself defined in terms of light. 'Beauty', wrote Plotinus, 'is rather a light that plays over the symmetry of things than the symmetry itself, and in this consists its charm.' It is this conception which finds exquisite expression in Byzantine art.

> Intus lux micat, atque bracteatum
> Sol sic sollicitatur ad lucanar,
> Fulvo ut concolor erret in metallo.
> Distinctum vario nitore marmor,
> Percurret cameram, solum, fenestras;
> Ac sub versicoloribus figuris
> Vernans herbida crusta sapphiratos
> Flectit per prasinum vitrum lapillos.[3]

Dr. T. Whittemore has shown how far the Church of Hagia Sophia may be regarded as an instrument of light: not merely in the glow and glitter of its mosaics, the sheen and reflection of its marbles, but also in the calculated effect of the rays of light falling across the microcosm of the nave.[4]

It is this same theory of beauty which finds new expression at the Renaissance. Marsilio Ficino finds that beauty 'does not lie in the material shadow, but in light and in grace of form, not in the murky mass, but in a certain shining proportion, not in dark and static

[1] On the connection between artistic contemplation and hypnosis see P. SOURIAU, *La suggestion dans l'art*, 1893; and A. COOMARASWAMY, *The Dance of Shiva*, 1918, p. 21. See also E. F. CARRITT, *Philosophies of Beauty*, Oxford 1931, p. 44.
[2] Plotinus, *Enneades*, 1, 6, 9.
[3] Apollinarius Sidonius, *Novae ecclesiae descriptio*, quoted HAVARD, *Histoire et philosophie des styles*, p. 97.
[4] Lecture at University College, London, March 12th, 1938.

weight, but in number and proportion',[1] and goes on: 'Pure colour, lights, voices, the shining of gold, the whiteness of silver, knowledge and the soul, these things do we call beautiful'. Whatever the relation between theory and practice, the quick extravert will find congenial art in the contemporary work of Mino da Fiesole, Agostino di Duccio and Botticelli, and in that of their successors Raphael, Tintoretto and Correggio. Such pictures and such sculpture generally have religious interest that is strong but not austere, beauty that is sensual but not gross, and colour and relief that are clear but not strong. They have too a hidden dramatic basis, since their iconography was deeply affected by the mystery plays of the late Middle Ages. All these qualities are likely to appeal to the extravert temperament and appeal they assuredly do. Men of each psychological type tend to admire the art produced by artists of the same type, and none more markedly than the quick extravert, since in them he can find escape from the burden of natural law.[2]

The quick introvert's tastes in the appreciation of works of art seem at first to be both eclectic and elusive. Reynolds describes him, not waiting for the slow process of deduction, but going at once, by what appears a kind of intuition, to the conclusion. 'Shall reason stand in the way and tell us we ought not to like what we know we do like and prevent us from feeling the full effect of this complicated exertion of art?' The quick introvert's primary taste is undoubtedly for decorative art, which

---

[1] *Epistolae*, I, 631.

[2] For a modern expression of this view see C. PERRIOLLAT, *Le Surnaturel dans l'art*, 1927, p. 4. 'Ainsi, hors du surnaturel, ni art, ni beauté . . . Si l'art n'est pas une réaction contre notre tendance naturelle à pénétrer de plus en plus par l'analyse dans la diversité, l'incohérence, l'instabilité des choses, vers la laideur et au contresens de la vie; si l'art n'est pas une révolte contre les servitudes et les dégradations que voudrait nous imposer notre nature matérielle . . . ce n'est plus qu'un n'importe quoi . . . qu'on ne sait plus comment définir et justifier, et qui ne répond plus à rien.'

has for him a lyric if inexpressible charm. In such work he especially loves natural forms intellectualized into an integrated pattern; Chinese art perfectly answers this need. It is, I think, exactly the same appeal that he finds in landscape paintings of a sort in which nature is made more formal and rhythmic than she generally appears; in the work, for example, of Claude and Wilson, Cotman and Francis Towne. He sees 'landscape as an end in itself — as pure form . . . and behind pure form lurks the mysterious significance that thrills to ecstasy'.[1] Similarly, the medieval art that combines observation and an intellectual code into a whole that is essentially decorative will appeal to him. He admires the arts of China and of France, that tend to have this basis of decorative design, and nearly always has a propensity for detesting the art of Germany,[2] that is only explicable because of a temperamental disharmony.

Since he is conscious not only of surface ornament but also of the form of the thing ornamented, he usually comes to appreciate architecture as the Mistress Art of all that he admires. William Morris may stand as an example. 'For him . . . the word architecture bore an immense, one might almost say a transcendental, meaning. Connected at a thousand points with all the other specific arts which ministered to it out of a thousand sources, it was itself the tangible expression of all the order, the comeliness, the sweetness, nay, even the mystery and the law, which sustain man's world and make human life what it is.'[3]

Moreover, any work of art in which the quick introvert is conscious of an appreciative yet intellectualized observation of nature may give him the peculiar aesthetic

---

[1] CLIVE BELL, *Art*, p. 208.   [2] e.g. Ibid., p. 139.
[3] MACKAIL, *Life of William Morris*, I, p. 78.

thrill he desiderates, and may therefore become part of his artistic world. He has no instinctive theories on the Beautiful and if circumstances force him to produce any they are simple and not far removed from fact. He knows instinctively whether an object is beautiful to him and cares very little what it is to other people. For the quick introvert is incapable of producing a complicated philosophy of aesthetics, and since he is so sensitive to visual impressions that he feels the emotions they arouse directly and not through the medium of words, he does not find it as easy as does the quick extravert to write about his aesthetic emotions.[1] So we find Mr. Clive Bell[2] discovering that the essential quality of the objects that provoke aesthetic emotions is 'significant form', which he defines back again as 'a combination of lines and colours ... that moves me aesthetically'.[3] Aquinas, however, had been through the scholastic mill; he refused to tread the accustomed ways, but, as an introvert should, linked theory afresh with thought when he claimed three essentials for beauty: integrity, since intelligence likes wholeness of being; proportion, since intelligence enjoys order; and brilliance and clearness, since intelligence loves light and comprehension. For him the entire sensible universe, as a symbol of the Divine reason, was perforce beautiful to the eye that could see it in relation to its Creator.[4]

Generally, however, if the quick introvert writes about art it is from the historic aspect, in an attempt to study

---

[1] It is probably significant that Shakespeare seems never to have reflected — or at least never to have attained expression for his reflections — on the nature of visual art.

[2] *Art*, 1916, pp. 8 and 12.

[3] For an interesting criticism of Mr. Clive Bell's point of view by a man of another temperament see R. H. WILENSKI, *The Modern Movement in Art*, 1935, p. 173.

[4] See BOSANQUET, p. 148.

cause and effect in the relation between a civilization and the art produced to satisfy its needs.

Ruskin, as has been ably shown by Professor Wilenski,[1] was a typical quick introvert, even to the point of mania, and perfectly illustrates the characteristic traits. Sculpture he only loved if it were architectural in character;[2] the representation of nature was for him the highest form of art;[3] and landscape was the kind of painting to which he instinctively turned. *Modern Painters* was begun as a dissertation on landscape without reference to any other kind of painting. Even in his attempts at aesthetic criticism he instinctively expressed the quick introvert's emphasis on social happiness: 'I believe the right question to ask respecting all ornament is simply this: "Was it done with enjoyment, was the carver happy while he was about it?"' He was always conscious of the relation between the artist and his public. Professor Wilenski complains: 'He always dragged in the spectator. He continually forgot that from the standpoint of the creative artist the spectator is not a man but a purse'.[4] But the artist of this temperament does not desire isolation from his public, and unless he is starving cares more for its appreciation than for its money.[5]

The slow extravert has perhaps less spontaneous appreciation of visual art than the man of any other type; and for this reason is the man most apt to lay down the law about it. When the first foundations of science

[1] *John Ruskin, an introduction to further study of his life and work*, 1933.
[2] 'I ought not to speak of sculpture because I have little pleasure in it when unconnected with architecture'. *Academy Notes*, 1857. Quoted WILENSKI, p. 225.
[3] 'All high art consists in the carving or painting of natural objects.' *Seven Lamps of Architecture*. Preface to second edition. Quoted WILENSKI, p. 215.
[4] *Seven Lamps*, v, par. 24. Quoted WILENSKI, p. 268.
[5] Cf. MACKAIL, *Life of William Morris*, II, p. 60: 'He (Morris) carried on his business as a manufacturer not because he wished to make money, but because he wished to make the things he manufactured.'

were being laid it was the slow extravert with his capacity for amassing facts who held the field. At the same time the first aesthetic philosophy was created under the same auspices. Instinctively the early thinkers concerned themselves with drama, with the conflict of man with men or circumstances or Fate, or with the 'mathematical' art of music rather than with the visual arts. When they did turn to such arts their thought was commonly limited by the mathematical conceptions which underlay all their science. Aristotle wrote: 'The main species of beauty are order, symmetry, definite limitation, and these are the chief properties that the mathematical sciences draw attention to'.[1] This Aristotelian concept of beauty as unity, symmetry, and order persisted through St. Augustine[2] and St. Gregory Nazianzen[3] into the scholastic philosophy of the Middle Ages.[4]

It is the slow extravert who tries to reduce beauty to laws of fact, though he may not always go so far as a writer of the fourth year of the French Republic, who declared: 'It remains to make a new application of mathematics to the arts to prove, directly and without consulting the eye, what forms are the most gracious, what scheme the most agreeable . . . For it is possible to reduce the unknown laws of beauty to a few fundamental principles, and once these principles are established, their application to particular instances will come into the sphere of geometry.'[5]

This predilection is the more natural because the slow extravert has as innate a liking for a straight line as the

---

[1] *Metaphysics*, 1078a, quoted BOSANQUET, *History of Aesthetics*, p. 33.
[2] *De vera religione*, CXXX.   [3] *Orat.*, XXII, § 15.
[4] See M. DE WULF, in *Revue Néo-scolastique*, XVII, 1909, p. 245.
[5] Décade, an. IV, & VIII, p. 270; the article is signed H. S. See JOAN EVANS, *Pattern*, 1931, II, 119.

quick introvert has for a curved one. Grant Allen[1] was probably right when he explained this liking on the grounds that a straight line is generally the mark of human handiwork. 'Straight lines are almost, if not quite, unknown in nature. Whenever we see a straight row of trees or plants, we know that they have been sown by the hand of man; whenever we come upon a straight stream of water, we recognize it as a canal of human construction ... As soon as the human race begins to use its hands for constructural purposes, the straight line is recognized as the most convenient boundary for many objects ... It has a regularity and perfection which naturally contrasts with the uneven handiwork of nature ... We must accordingly allow a certain aesthetic value — intellectual rather than sensuous — to the straight line; which none can doubt except that class of mystical thinkers, who consider merely the most complex artistic developments instead of beginning with the simplest elements.'

It follows that the slow extravert is always ready to acknowledge a geometrical basis for his art. Michelangelo prescribed for his pupil Marco del Pino da Siena 'that he should always make a figure Pyramidal, Serpentlike, and multiplied by one, two, and three',[2] and even Hogarth was forced to invent a 'Line of Beauty' that makes a weak support for a theory of aesthetics. Headed by Fechner, the experimental psychologists of this school are content to confine themselves to preferences in geometrical figures. Fechner's chief researches in pictures were confined to the subject of their external measurements[3] and the chief discovery of all his experiments was that a rectangle in the propor-

---

[1] *Physiological Aesthetics*, p. 169.
[2] LAMOZZO, *On Painting*, trans. Haydock, Oxford, 1598.
[3] *Vorschule der Æsthetik*, II, 179.

tions of the 'Golden Section'[1] was more universally pleasing to the eye than another rectangle. Similarly certain psychologists who have followed Fechner in trying to reduce aesthetics to an experimental basis have been content to discover a general tendency to choose some asymmetrical division of line or space, and to conclude 'that the development of taste leads to a preference of proportion to symmetry'.[2] Benedetto Croce[3] aptly calls such casting of figures the astrology of aesthetics.

This connection with mathematics is not the only attempt made by the slow extravert thinker to connect the mystery of art with something he understands. Xenophon reminds us in the *Memorabilia* that Socrates connected the beauty of any object with its fitness for purpose, and the slow extravert is often tempted to confuse beauty with utility. Quintilian found that 'nunquam vera species ab utilitate dividitur'.[4] The philosopher Hume considered that the canon of utility was applicable to '. . . tables, chairs, scritoires, chimneys, coaches, sadles, ploughs, and indeed to every work of art; it being an universal rule, that their beauty is chiefly deriv'd from their utility, and from their fitness for that purpose, to which they are destin'd . . . 'Tis evident, that nothing renders a field more agreeable

---

[1] i.e. a figure determined by a ratio of its sides such that the less is to the greater as the greater is to the sum of the two; a ratio roughly satisfied by 8 : 13 or 21 : 34. See *Vorschule der Aesthetik*, 1876, p. 190.

[2] See WITMER, Zur Experimentalen Aesthetik Einfacher Raumlicher Form Verhälttnisse in *Phil. Studien*, IX, 1893, and R. P. ANGIER, *The Aesthetics of Unequal Division*. An earlier (and less scientific) writer on the subject was Henry Home of Kames who, in his *Elements of Criticism* first published in 1761, compares the beauties of a square, and a parallelogram and a triangle (ed. Boyd, 1865, p. 113). A more subtle theory is the 'dynamic symmetry' of Mr. JAY HAMBIDGE, which finds full expression in his periodical, *The Diagonal*, 1919-20. His book, *Dynamic Symmetry in Composition* (Cambridge, Mass., 1923), shows the rather disappointing results of using his theory as a basis for modern art.

[3] *Aesthetic*, trans. Ainslie, 1909, p. 181.   [4] *Or. Inst.*, VIII, 3.

than its fertility, and that scarce any advantages of ornament or situation will be able to equal this beauty ... I know not but a plain, overgrown with furze and broom, may be, in itself, as beautiful as a hill covere'd with vines or olive trees; tho' it will never appear so to one, who is acquainted with the value of each. But this is a beauty merely of imagination, and has no foundation in what appears to the senses.'[1]

Quite recently the utilitarian view has received a fresh extension at the hands of an economist.[2] 'An essential element in art-value is fitness for function, and this includes not only technical fitness but economic fitness. Economic fitness includes two ideas: (1) that in the production of a work of art there should be a just and fitting relation between the cost incurred in terms of effort and materials, and the degree of importance, dignity and nobility of the ends which the work is to serve; (2) that there should similarly be a fitting relation between the cost of the work and the level of well-being or purchasing power of the persons for whose use it is intended.'

The utilitarian point of view causes critics to include much extraneous matter within the sphere of art and to judge it by other than aesthetic standards. Fergusson,[3] for example, included such arts as heating, ventilation, joinery and gastronomy in his scheme, and in a statistical table of artistic values put eloquence at the very top of the list. Even individual buildings he marked like examination papers, awarding the Pyramids 20, Cologne Cathedral 22, Rheims 24 and the Parthenon 24.

---

[1] *Treatise on Human Nature*, Bk. II, Pt. II, sect. v. Guyau is a more recent philosopher who has striven to identify utility with beauty.
[2] H. LLEWELLYN SMITH, *The Economic Laws of Art Production*, 1924, p. 133.
[3] J. FERGUSSON, *An Historical Enquiry into the true principles of Beauty in Art* ... 1849, p. 140.

Another aspect of this inability to judge works of art on purely aesthetic grounds is a preoccupation with their moral significance. Jonathan Richardson found that 'a picture is useful to instruct and improve our mind, to excite proper sentiments and reflections . . . a history is preferable to a landscape, sea piece, animals, fruit, flower, or any other still life . . . They cannot improve the mind, they excite no noble sentiments'.[1] A modern philosopher[2] finds that 'Foremost among causes which have contributed to the formation of an idealistic art appears to stand the subordination of art to some extraneous purpose of an impressive exceptional character . . . commemorative, hieratic, generally religious, royal or patriotic.'

The slow extravert is usually willing to follow the first great philosopher of his temperament, Aristotle, in considering art to be mainly mimetic. He has a real liking for what Mr. Clive Bell defines as descriptive painting: 'that is, painting in which forms are not used as objects of emotion, but as means of suggesting emotion or conveying information'.[3] M. Vialle expresses the slow extravert's view when he says:[4] 'Le principe de l'art est peut-être dans l'aptitude qu'ont les images à provoquer, bien que généralement avec une intensité moindre, les mêmes sentiments que la réalité'. So, he suggests, there is a pleasure in evoking memories through art and thus in living through dead joys and sorrows in an attentuated form. Much the same point of view was expressed by Byron when he wrote: 'I know nothing of painting and detest it, unless it reminds

[1] Quoted E. W. MANWARING. *Italian Landscape in 18th-century England*, p. 23.
[2] E. BULLOUGH, 'Psychical Distance as a factor in Art and an Aesthetic Principle' in *British Journal of Psychology*, v, 1912-13. (Cambridge 1913), p. 100.
[3] *Art*, p. 16.
[4] *Le désir du néant*, p. 95.

me of something I have seen or think it possible to see'.[1]

I have already written of the slow extravert's tendency to treat his room as an autobiographical museum, and this tendency, whether applied to the history of the individual or the nation, leads him to prefer portraits, topographical pictures and illustrations of all sorts: exactly the pictures classified by Mr. Clive Bell as 'descriptive painting'. Barry in 1775 wrote[2] that 'History painting and sculpture should be the main views of any people desirous of gaining honour by the arts. These are the tests by which the national character will be tried in after ages . . . these are the great sources from whence all the rivulets of art flow, and from whence only is derived the vigour and character that truly ennobles them.' This view of art as historical documentation is not nowadays held by professional art-critics; but a visit to any Royal Academy exhibition will prove that it still exists in this country.

In portraits and historical pictures the desire for 'associations' haunts the slow extravert:[3] he prefers an ugly portrait of a known person to a fine one of an unknown, and a mediocre picture that is signed to a good one that is anonymous. For the slow extravert who has received a classical education the remarks made by Richard Payne Knight in 1805[4] are still true:

'Ruined buildings, with fragments of sculptured walls and broken columns, the mouldering remnants of obsolete taste and fallen magnificence, afford pleasure to

---

[1] In a letter to Murray, quoted H. E. A. FURST, *The New Anecdotes of Painters and Painting* [1926], p. 41.
[2] J. BARRY, *An Inquiry into the real and imaginary obstructions to the acquisition of the Arts in England*, p. 132.
[3] Fechner was being true to type when he made his chief contribution to aesthetic thought the development of the idea of the 'Associations-princip'.
[4] *Analytical Enquiry into the Principles of Taste*, p. 192.

every learned beholder, imperceptible to the ignorant, and wholly independent of their real beauty ... More especially when discovered in countries of ancient celebrity, renowned in history for learning, arts, or empire. The mind is led by the view of them into the most pleasing trains of ideas; and the whole scenery around receives an accessory character; which is commonly called *classical*; as the ideas, which it excites, associated themselves with those which the mind has previously received from the writings called classic.'[1]

It is not easy for a man of another temperament, who is sensitive to 'the disinterested emotion of delight felt through contemplation',[2] to understand the aesthetic processes of the slow extravert. For this delight is very rarely felt by the slow extravert; his tendency to amplification denies him that intensity of feeling which simplification alone can bring to art. None the less he will rarely allow that there are varieties of aesthetic experience of which he is not qualified to judge. Proudhon exceptionally admitted: 'Je n'ai pas l'intuition esthétique; je manque de ce sentiment primesautier de goût qui fait juger d'emblée si une chose est belle ou non'; but this did not prevent him from writing a lengthy treatise *Du principe de l'art et de sa destination sociale*.[3]

An interesting analysis by a psychologist of this temperament of his own feelings in face of such a building as a cathedral,[4] bring out this non-aesthetic point of view. He found that they could be analysed, in a diminishing scale of intensity, as based on the interest of human

---

[1] An excellent example of the attempt to translate visual into literary art is provided by SHAFTESBURY's 'Tablature of the judgment of Hercules' in *Characteristicks*, Treatise VII (1723 ed., III, p. 345).

[2] YRJÖ HIRN.

[3] 1865, p. 10. He emphasizes the social aims of art, decrees that it must be a collective product, and finds that only content matters while form is negligible.

[4] H. STURT, 'Art and Personality' in *Personal Idealism*, 1902, p. 296.

association, the interest of workmanship, the interest of nationality, the interest of organic character, and the interest of the vitality of the parts.[1]

This tendency to confuse the aesthetic impression made by a work of art with the associated ideas evoked by its subject is nowhere more clearly expressed than in recent psycho-analytic works on aesthetics.[2] M. Baudouin gives an account of the reactions of a patient of his before Dürer's well-known engraving of St. Jerome. St. Jerome reminded her of Goethe's Faust, and of a personal problem that had occupied her mind when she was reading it; the window recalled to her a holiday she had passed in the mountains, the cushions an Eastern harem, the death's head a jewel of similar shape, the lion a bad dream, and so on: and a slow extravert might well find it hard to believe that none of this associational process enters into a purely aesthetic sensation.[3] The question is complicated by the existence of 'surrealist art' which is composed as an expression of such associated ideas.[4] One of its protagonists, M. André Breton, has defined surrealism[5] as 'Automatisme psychique pur par lequel on se propose d'exprimer ... le fonctionnement réel de la pensée. Dictée de la pensée, en l'absence de tout contrôle exercé par la raison, en dehors de toute préoccupation esthétique ou morale.' Fortunately an art which declares itself without aesthetic intention lies outside the scope of this book.

[1] This last is a form of Empathy: see below, p. 59.

[2] See especially C. BAUDOUIN, *Psychanalyse de l'Art*, 1929. A similar tendency is earlier evident in GRANT ALLEN, *Physiological Aesthetics*, 1877, p. 222.

[3] For a different sort of associated idea, in which seeing a picture brings a piece of music to the mind, or having music in the mind brings significance to a picture, see VERNON LEE and C. ASTRUTHER THOMSON, *Beauty and Ugliness*, 1912, p. 280 *et seq.*

[4] M. C. BAUDOUIN has pointed out that *dadaisme*, its progenitor, was created at Zurich in 1916 in a strongly psycho-analytic medium. *Psychanalyse de l' Art*, p. 1214

[5] *Qu'est ce que le Surréalisme?* Brussels [1934].

The slow extravert has other artistic pleasures that are peculiarly his own. He generally belongs to the 'motor' type,[1] that is especially sensible to the pleasures of muscular exertion. He therefore finds a genuine aesthetic pleasure in terms of muscular stress.[2] It is true to say that such a man enjoys in art either muscular action or the straight lines which are the result of muscular action upon nature. Mr. Berenson has made a skilled analysis of this enjoyment of muscular action in relation to a group of wrestlers.[3] 'Now if a way could be found of conveying to us the realization of movement without the confusion and the fatigue of the actuality, we should be getting out of the wrestlers more than they themselves can give us — the heightening of vitality which comes to us whenever we keenly realize life, such as the actuality itself would give us, *plus* the greater effectiveness of the heightening brought about by the clearer, intenser and less fatiguing realization. This is precisely what the artist who succeeds in representing movement achieves: making us realize it as we never can actually, he gives us a heightened sense of capacity, and whatever is in the actuality enjoyable, he allows us to enjoy at our leisure.'

It is this pleasure, whether enjoyed directly through painting and sculpture, or by analogy through architecture,[4] which finds philosophic expression in the doctrine of *Einfuhlung* or Empathy, that endows the lines of the thing perceived with movement, reflected

---

[1] See VERNON LEE and C. ANSTRUTHER THOMSON, *Beauty and Ugliness*, 1912, p. 24, where the opinion of Professor Groos is cited.

[2] GRANT ALLEN (*Physiological Aesthetics*, 1877, p. 34) equally ascribes a purely physical basis to aesthetic enjoyment, but is rather more scientific about it. 'Aesthetic pleasure may be provisionally defined as the subjective concomitant of the normal amount of activity not directly connected with life-serving function, in the peripheral end-organs of the cerebrospinal nervous system.'

[3] *Florentine Painters*, p. 50.

[4] This aspect probably finds its first expression in the Vitruvian parallels between architecture and the human figure.

in the imagination and to some degree even in the body, of the man who perceives it. The lines[1] *topple, strive, rise* and *arrest* each other; and the spectator derives from the life with which he endows them a vicarious sense of strength and energy. The experience — which is not, I think, shared in any great degree by men of other types[2] — is best described at first-hand.

'The secondary, or human emotions connected with Gothic churches ... are explicable by the fact that acutely pointed arches are perceived by an adjustment which feels as if the breath of both lungs were running simultaneously upwards in a point, with a consequent strain and contraction the reverse of that expansion, which is accompanied by the sense of serenity and fellowship with the non-ego. Moreover, the act of breathing far higher up, both by its unusualness and by the strain it imposes, produces a state of being analogous to that of solitary and Quixotic resolves, forced upon us by the very nature of our surroundings.'[3]

If this sense of transferred movement can be derived from architecture, it can be yet more strongly experienced from pictures that portray human figures. Aristotle in the second chapter of the *Poetics* declares that 'men in action' are the objects imitated not only by dramatic or narrative poetry but by all the Fine Arts.[4] To many of his readers this has seemed a hard saying; but it is in fact true to the slow extravert's conception of visual art, since from the pictures or sculpture of men in action they derive their strongest aesthetic stimulus. So Vernon Lee writes of her enjoyment of a Rubens battle scene: 'a

[1] See VERNON LEE, *The Beautiful*, Cambridge, 1913, especially chapter x.
[2] For an interesting criticism of it by one of another type see E. D. PUFFER, *The Psychology of Beauty*, Cambridge, Mass., 1905, p. 118.
[3] VERNON LEE and C. ANSTRUTHER THOMSON, op. cit., p. 195. This section is signed C.A.T.
[4] See S. H. BUTCHER, *Aristotle's Theory of Poetry and Fine Arts*, 1908, p. 115.

distinct feature in this pleasure is a sense of pushing forward and of concentration far greater than a real horse or real man would have: a dynamic *unity of strenuousness*'.[1]

It is the slow extravert who maintains the distinction between the Fine Arts and the lesser arts that was first established by Aristotle. The true distinction, I think, which the slow extravert makes by this classification is between the arts that are capable of dynamic composition and those that are not. Certainly his idea of giving the decorative arts a patent of nobility as fine arts always consists in endowing them with a dynamic composition: the wall paintings of the later Renaissance are an example. Baroque architecture was an attempt to ennoble the art of building by treating it dynamically. Moreover, 'fine' art demands complexity and greatness in the social group for whom it is composed. Ornament, like the lyric, may flower as easily in a lesser compass, but 'fine art' demands the perfected organization in which the slow extravert, with his innate gift for administration, tends to dominate society. Its very existence glorifies his type. For him the detached work of fine art is what matters; and for him the classical work of art — inexploitable to the quick extravert and a trifle savourless to the quick introvert — has a profound appeal. He may no longer swear by the Apollo Belvedere and the Laocoön, who are out of fashion, but he will have found substitutes for them in less hackneyed works of classical art,[2] and in the works of modern sculptors

---

[1] *Beauty and Ugliness*, p. 282. The italics are hers.

[2] William Morris was not an extravert and rather disliked classical art; but his criticism of it emphasizes the qualities in it that appeal to the extravert. 'In the perfect art of Greece the tendency was so decidedly towards fact of all kinds that it could only give a very low place to ornament that had not a definite meaning. In short, this perfect art preferred blankness to richness.' *History of Pattern Designing*, p. 8.

who constrain the spectator to follow the feeling and action of the person represented.[1]

In ordinary life, however courageous he may be, the slow extravert is haunted by fear; and in the contemplation of the Sublime in any art he has this emotion at its most exquisite yet devoid of any interested quality. Burke, in his definition of the Sublime as including Greatness, Infinity, Succession, Uniformity and Difficulty, rightly endows it with a slow extravert's idea of beauty. He further explains its appeal to the slow extravert's innate sense of personal grandeur. 'Whatever tends to raise in man his own opinion, produces a sort of swelling and triumph, that is extremely grateful to the human mind. And this swelling is never more perceived, nor operates with more force, than when without danger we are conversant with terrible objects — the mind always claiming to itself some of the dignity and importance of the things which it contemplates.'

These qualities the slow extravert will find chiefly in sculpture and in such architecture as that of ancient Egypt. There, too, he will not be troubled overmuch by the mystery of colour, but (like Winckelmann) can find beauty not in colour but in shape. He will find the same *sainte horreur* in negro sculpture, in the primitive art of South America, and in the modern art that takes its inspiration from such sources.

The remaining aesthetic pleasure that is stronger in the slow extravert than in other men is that derived from pure technical skill. A competent person himself, he admires competence in others and therefore appreciates *tours de force* of every kind: carvings in hard stone,

---

[1] Cf. RODIN, *L'Art*, Entretiens réuins par P. Gsell, 1911, p. 72. 'J'ai toujours essayé de rendre les sentiments intérieurs par la mobilité des muscles ... Le statuaire contraint, pour ainsi dire, le spectateur à suivre le développement d'un acte à travers un personnage.'

filigree in recalcitrant metal, and any form of art which he knows to be difficult.

> Oui, l'œuvre sort plus belle
> D'une forme au travail
> Rebelle,
> Vers, marbre, onyx, émail . . .

He would agree with John Stuart Mill, that 'Art is an endeavour after perfection in execution';[1] and is apt unconsciously to identify the *virtuoso* and the artist.

The slow introvert, who strives to understand so much, rarely turns his mind to the understanding of concrete works of visual art. It is entirely characteristic that Plato[2] in the *Republic* should desiderate a beauty of style and a harmony and grace that depend upon simplicity, and in the *Timaeus* should add a proportion that links the work of art with the universal and moral order, with no further discussion of the aesthetic qualities of visual art. It is equally characteristic that for him music should be the dominant art; poetry the next, and the visual arts no more than the vaguest background.

It is not often that the slow introvert will express an opinion about a work of visual art; yet if its sudden beauty forces him to do so, his canons of proportion and relation and his natural sincerity make him a critic to be respected. It is a characteristic of almost diagnostic validity that he does not write about the visual arts, unless he is a practising artist; then he writes as a craftsman rather than a critic.

The individual is apt to find a peculiarly congenial quality in works of art produced by men of his own temperament. Delacroix, who might stand as the type

---

[1] Cf. GRANT ALLEN, *Physiological Aesthetics*, p. 190, and SAINT-SAËNS, 'La difficulté vaincue est elle-même une beauté'.
[2] *Republic*, III, 401.

of the slow extravert artist, admired (and sometimes even copied) the works of Goya, Rowlandson, Rubens, Ingres, Constable and Lawrence;[1] and I should conceive all these artists to have been of the same temperament as himself. Curiously often the man who is conscious of this spontaneous liking will describe it in terms of friendly affinity. William Morris wrote[2] of the Gothic Churches of Northern France that they were 'the grandest, the most beautiful, the kindest and most loving of all the buildings that the earth has ever borne'. The late Professor of Poetry at Oxford writes:[3]

'Some poets are more *friendly* than others. I like to think that among the friendly poets are some of the greatest. The most friendly of them all is the first of them, Chaucer . . . After Chaucer . . . the most friendly of them is, beyond a doubt, the greatest of them, Shakespeare . . . After Chaucer and Shakespeare for friendliness we must go, I think, to two Scots — to Burns and "Sir Walter".' Such frankly subjective criticism is revealing because — as here — it is apt to group together writers and artists of similar temperament.

A man will always tend to have a primary attraction towards the art produced by men of like temperament with himself; so the slow extravert Daumier had a passion for Rembrandt and Rubens,[4] and David — a man of the same temperament — admired Van Ostade, Teniers, Subleyras and Rembrandt,[5] all slow extraverts likewise. Yet a man may also experience a secondary attraction to the work of men of another type. A slow introvert, if he be sad or tired, may find the

[1] See R. ESCHOLIER, *Delacroix*, 3 vols., 1926.
[2] Quoted MACKAIL, *Life of William Morris*, 1, p. 96.
[3] H. W. GARROD, *The Study of Poetry*, Oxford, 1935.
[4] R. ESCHOLIER, *Daumier*, 1913, p. 11.
[5] P. M. TURNER and C. H. COLLINS BAKER, *Stories of the French Artists*, 1909, p. 301.

work of another slow introvert depressing, and may turn to that of a man of a quicker form of his own temperament.[1] A slow extravert in like case may turn to the work of a quick extravert, and find there either the human gaiety or the mystical reassurance that he needs. In his turn the quick extravert (though rarely) may seek reassurance from those who are closer to actuality than himself; so Van Gogh writes: 'I feel always a great attraction for the figures either of the English draughtsmen or of the English authors, because of their Monday-morning-like soberness, and studied simplicity and prosaicness and analysis, as something solid and strong that can give us strength in days when we feel weak'.[2] So the quick introvert may find in the gracious calm of the work of the slow introvert the peace that his over-stimulated mind demands. Thus the quick introvert William Morris had an especial admiration for the work of the melancholic Van Eyck and Holbein,[3] and Corot enjoyed and even imitated Vermeer of Delft. Manet said of Velasquez: 'Il ne m'a pas étonné, mais il m'a ravi'.[4] Such secondary attractions, however, are often symptomatic of fatigue or stress, and are less characteristic and more variable than the attraction of like to like.

---

[1] His natural antipathy for quick extravert work never varies. Velasquez said to Salvator Rosa: 'Raphael, I must confess, does not please me at all'. Quoted H. E. A. FURST, *The New Anecdotes of Painters and Painting* [1926], p. 35.
[2] *Letters to his Brother*, I, p. 536.
[3] MACKAIL, *Life of William Morris*, II, p. 272.
[4] E. MOREAU NÉLATON, *Manet raconté par lui-même*, 1926, I, p. 72.

CHAPTER IV

THE PRACTISING ARTIST

Dans le siècle présent comme dans les anciens, aujourd'hui
comme autrefois, les hommes forts et bien portants se
partagent, chacun suivant son goût et son tempérament,
les divers territoires de l'art, et s'y exercent en pleine
liberté suivant la loi fatale du travail attrayant
C. BAUDELAIRE, *Curiosités esthétiques*

I

BEFORE we turn to the difficult question of the relation
of temperament to art in the case of the true creative
artist, we must briefly consider one of the central
problems of the history of art: the influences that create
the style of a nation or of an age. Environment may have
an influence, but that influence may seem to exercise
itself in contrary fashion. Catalonia is a land of noble
mountains and fertile plains, bathed in a lucid atmosphere that lends alike to foreground and to distance a
harmonious intensity of colour: yet the great medieval
School of Catalan painters made hardly any use of
landscape backgrounds, but are notable for their
grounds of ornamental gold or plain colour. It was not
until the Catalan School was influenced by that of
Flanders — from the scenic point of view one of the
dullest districts in Europe — that landscape backgrounds
came into use. Similarly naturalistic decoration tends
to be produced in civilizations courtly, urban or
enclosed enough for distance to lend enchantment to
men's view of nature.[1]

Setting aside the reasons of geographical contacts,

[1] See JOAN EVANS, *Nature in Design*, Oxford, 1933.

economic conditions, and historical circumstances which do not here concern us — though they are rightly the preoccupations of the art-historian — we are left with certain phenomena which can only be explained in terms of the influence of one temperament upon others.

Some men, though not themselves capable of direct artistic creation, may in virtue of riches or authority be able to make other men express their tastes. The slow extravert, though not usually finding instinctive expression in terms of visual art, will none the less through his gift for domination often succeed in thus imposing his tastes upon the art of others. The Pharaohs thus imposed a paranoid art upon ancient Egypt; the Great Pyramid, for example, in greatness of size, angularity of line and simplicity of design, as in its intent to glorify and immortalize a monarch, is a perfect example of slow extravert architecture.[1] The founders of the Order of Cîteaux—paranoid in their austerity, their fanaticism and their genius for organization — succeeded in imposing a slow extravert style of architecture upon all the houses of the Order built in the Romanesque period.[2] Whether it be studied in France at Fontenay and Pontigny, in Catalonia at Poblet and Santes Creus, in England at Furness and Fountains, the Cistercian tradition is essentially the same. When the Cistercian St. Bernard inveighed against the architecture of the Order of Cluny[3] it was not merely a religious fanatic

[1] L. MARCH PHILLIPS, *The Works of Man*, 1932 (1st edition 1911), p. 8: 'a uniform, solid triangle of masonry, mechanically accurate and utterly expressionless in its dead monotony, without any intelligible purpose . . . save the stupid and ignoble one of hiding a wretched corpse within its bowels — that, I believe, is an architectural phenomenon absolutely without a parallel'.

[2] Cf. the passage in the Consuetudines of 1134 on the illumination of manuscripts: 'Litterae unius coloris fiant et non depictae', § lxxx.

[3] *Apologia* addressed to Guillaume, Abbot of Saint Thierry, *c.* 1125. MIGNE, *Patrologia Latina*, CLXXXII, col. 914. Translated in G. G. COULTON, *Mediaeval Garner*, 1910, p. 71.

inveighing against those who follow his religion in a less austere form, but the slow extravert reiterating his eternal criticism of quick introvert art.

'Why dost thou make so fair that which will soon be made so foul? Why lavish bright hues upon that which must needs be trodden underfoot? What avail these comely forms in places where they are defiled with customary dust? . . . So many and so marvellous are the varieties of divers shapes on every hand, that we are more tempted to read in the marble than in our books, and to spend the whole day in wondering at these things rather than in meditating the law of God. For God's sake, if men are not ashamed of these follies, why at least do they not shrink from the expense?'

Perhaps the building most typical of the slow extravert mind is the Escorial, reflecting the temperament of Philip II who ordered and approved its designs and paid for its construction. Built in fulfilment of a vow made in expiation of the destruction of a church dedicated to St. Lawrence, it is shaped like the gridiron on which the saint was martyred, with a rectangular outline only broken on one side where the Royal apartments project like the handle of the gridiron. Its granite is hewn from the mountain on which it stands. It is so vast that it is said to have a hundred miles of corridors and so plain that its exterior sides are like cliffs pierced by the windows of troglodyte dwellings. Even the towers at the angles do not project but are flush with the walls; the plain rectangular windows have neither moulding nor cornice. Where a classical order is employed it is the simplest Doric. As originally approved by Philip II it had little colour and less ornament. It holds under one roof a monastery, a great church, a palace and the mausoleum of the king who built it and of all his progeny.

The paranoid theist's sense of sin and apprehension of death there find characteristic expression. It is a place of dread.

Patronage of the simplest kind is always apt to turn an artist's work for a time into uncongenial channels. Holbein was a portrait painter with a slow introvert's interest in psychology, but he had to design jewels for Henry VIII. In the paintings of Velasquez it is not hard to distinguish between the pictures he painted with gusto and the pictures he painted to order. The few religious pictures which he painted as such, and did not transmute into scenes of contemporary life, must be treated as illustrations of the law of supply and demand and not as characteristic expressions of his art.

These are instances of the domination of an individual or of a small organized group. There is also a far more elusive domination of art by the predominant type in the civilization of the time. It is not only the influence of oriental and Mudejar art that lends a quick introvert quality to fourteenth-century decoration, but also the taste of the House of Valois and of a Court that modelled itself upon them. It is not only the rediscovery of Pompeii that imposed the neo-classic style on England, but also the taste of the English aristocracy, dominated by a caste of slow extravert administrators, that felt at home in a room so severe that it looks its best without inhabitants.

Fashion and economic conditions may easily drive an artist into a *genre* which he would not otherwise have chosen; Michelangelo was never meant to be a painter,[1] nor Piranesi to design chimney pieces. Degas might have been one of the great portrait painters of Europe, had

[1] For a good account of the incongruous subjects forced upon him see BERENSON, *Florentine Painters of the Renaissance*, p. 90.

the taste of his day permitted it.[1] The curiously constant
demand for portraits in England — a country which
tends to be dominated by a slow extravert tradition —
has driven many an artist into portraiture who might
have been happier in landscape,[2] just as the constant
demand for religious pictures in Spain and Italy has
driven many a fine portraitist into religious art; witness
the figures of donors that are often the best painted part
of religious pictures of the fifteenth and sixteenth
centuries.[3] It follows, therefore, that in any psychological investigation an artist's work must be judged not
by that part of it which belongs to the normal and
general art of his time, but by that which is especially
and essentially his own.

II

Obviously the artist's temperamental relation to
art is a development of the taste of the ordinary individual towards works of art, since art is the positive
expression of what a man finds beautiful.[4] Yet this is not
all; the spiritual truth of a work of art is truth not only
to the artist's vision of the fleeting appearances of
exterior nature, but also to that enduring inner nature
that we call Temperament. 'Le style, c'est de l'homme
même.' Even Reynolds, writing in an age which tended
to recognize only one taste, and that classical and

[1] The idea that he was a slow extravert is confirmed by his admiration for
Ingres and Delacroix; he made a collection of the works of both these artists.
[2] Reynolds, for example, since he lived in an age that gave first place to animal
life, spoke almost apologetically of landscape (Third Discourse).
[3] An instance is NICHOLAS FROMENT's *Altarpiece of the Burning Bush.*
[4] Cf. REYNOLDS, Seventh Discourse: 'Genius and taste in their common
acceptation, appear to be very nearly related; the difference lies only in this, that
genius has superadded to it a habit or power of execution.'

generalized, could declare: '. . . It is in the works of art as in the characters of men. The faults or defects of some men seem to become them, when they appear to be the natural growth, and of a piece with the rest of their character. A faithful picture of a mind, though it be not of the most elevated kind, though it be irregular, wild and incorrect, yet if it be marked with that spirit and firmness which characterize works of genius, will claim attention, and be more striking than a combination of excellencies that do not seem to unite well together. . . .'[1]

Temperament plays its part even in the question of medium. Water colours and tempera, that must be executed swiftly, are media for men with quick reactions: black and white is as obviously the medium for the slow introvert. Pastel was invented for the quick extravert; and monumental, as opposed to decorative, sculpture was probably the creation of the slow extravert. Yet temperament affects even the use of an uncongenial medium. Gainsborough was, I think, a quick extravert, and it is significant to find Laurence Binyon writing of his 'marvellously light and fresh and spontaneous' brush-work, that Gainsborough treats oil paints 'almost as if they were water colours'.[2] Michelangelo, a slow extravert, paints as a man whose *métier* is sculpture. The slow extravert thinkers have driven the visual arts into specific *genres*, and it would seem natural that each temperament should have found a *genre* for itself; it is easy to predict the sentimental picture, whether of a saint or a pretty woman, for the quick extravert, the dramatic subject picture, topographical art, and the official portrait for the slow extravert, and landscape and

---

[1] Fifth Discourse. He instances Salvator Rosa, Rubens and Poussin.
[2] *Landscape in English Art and Poetry*, p. 71.

71

still life for the quick introvert.[1] Such predictions will find a certain justification in fact, if the essential and not the whole work of the painter is considered, but the choosing of the 'essential' is a subjective matter; and it does not follow that any one critic's opinion will be generally accepted.

III

The quick extravert nearly always brings a supernatural quality into his art: for him art has neither to represent nor to interpret nature, but to transcend it. Burne-Jones writes: 'I mean by a picture a beautiful romantic dream of something that never was, never will be — in a light better than any light that ever shone — in a land no one can define or remember, only desire. . . .'[2]

I have already spoken of the double trend in the quick extravert temperament, towards worldly elegance on the one hand and mystical religion on the other. This double element is plainly reflected in his art. The two *genres* in which he excels are boudoir art on the one hand and ecstatic art on the other. In any *genre* he has a curious tendency to depict people of his own temperament; were the personages of Raphael's *Sistine Madonna* or his *Tommaso Inghirami* to come as out-patients a skilled physician would soon have them diagnosed. He does not usually create new schemes; even Reynolds,

---

[1] Chardin is an admirable instance; for the last twenty-five years of his life he painted nothing but still life.

[2] Quoted Mrs. Laurence Binyon, *The Mind of the Artist*, 1909, p. 9. Cf. Blake: 'Shall painting be confined to the sordid drudgery of facsimile representations of merely mortal and perishing substances, and not be as poetry and music are, elevated into its own proper sphere of invention and visionary conception?' Ibid., p. 12.

who after the fashion of his day admired Raphael, had to admit that one of his excellencies lay in the 'skilful accommodation of other men's conceptions to his own purposes'. I do not know how often Monet painted his water-lilies; he is said to have painted the same haystack eighty-three times.[1] But under the stress of some emotional ecstasy the quick extravert may transform a given scheme — as El Greco sometimes did — into something new and strange. The quick extravert's vision of actuality is too unreal for him to be a great portraitist; El Greco's portraits (when they are not entirely subordinated to a religious scheme) are monotonous enough to suggest self-portraiture; and there is a curious artificiality about the portraits by Lucas Cranach. But when it is a matter of representing the idea of herself that a pretty woman plays before an appreciative public, the quick extravert is the first to do justice to the histrionic effort. It took the Great War to break the tradition of English beauty established in the pictures of Gainsborough, if indeed it has yet been broken; and it is characteristic that some of his best portraits are of 'Perdita' Robinson, Signora Bacelli, Kitty Fisher and Miss Dalrymple, the great demi-mondaines of his day. Emma Hamilton's 'Attitudes' were probably among the most enchanting mimes that a hysteric has ever performed: and it is significant that paintings of them are the most successful of George Romney's work. This particular aptitude probably accounts for the apparent preponderance of such artists as painters of women in England from about 1770 until 1914, if not until the present day.

So long as the life of pleasure dominates any society, so long will the 'boudoir' art of the quick extravert, that

[1] H. E. A. FURST, *The New Anecdotes of Painters and Painting* [1926], p. 84.

73

forms a decorative parallel to such portraits, be an element of considerable commercial importance in the art of its time. The French art of the Régence and of the time of Louis XV remains the perfect example; but seventeenth-century Venice and *fin de siècle* England could provide as characteristic if less exquisite examples of the *genre*. Greuze's advice, 'Soyez piquant si vous ne pouvez pas être vrai',[1] admirably sums up its intention,

In his religious pictures, as in his religious thought, the quick extravert artist escapes from 'la détresse de n'être pas Dieu' by acting as God and breaking the laws of nature. He contradicts the fundamental law of gravity by adopting a levitational scheme; his figures are either definitely soaring, or so lightly poised that they do not truly rest upon the ground.[2] The tendency is early evident (though with full justification in the subject) in such Greek sculpture as the Nike of Paeonius and the Ganymede of Leochares, and with less justification in the lightly-poised statues of the Praxitelean school. I have already spoken of the quick extravert's love of the 'hypnotic' quality of a broken, glittering, golden surface; this is often combined with the levitational scheme. Both appear in the frescoes of the early second century from Dura-Europos; both recur in many Byzantine mosaics.[3] Botticelli's paintings show this factitious lightness of foot:[4] it is this which helps to give his pictures (to introvert eyes) a morbid quality in spite of their vigorous

---

[1] Quoted H. E. A. FURST, *The New Anecdotes of Painters and Painting* [1926], p. 5.

[2] For flying delusions in hysteria see JANET, *De l'angoisse à l'extase*, 1926-8, I, p. 87.

[3] It seems that both may be derived from the Mazdaean art of Iran. See DIEZ, *Byzantine Mosaics in Greece*, p. 29; R. HINKS, *Carolingian Art*, 1935, p. 37. Curious *pastiches* — conscious or unconscious — of Byzantine style may be found among the drawings of morbid hysterics. See for example, H. PRINZHORN, *Bildnerei der Geisteskranken*, 2nd ed. Berlin, 1923, p. 116.

[4] His sudden conversion, and the religious pictures of his last phase, are equally characteristic of the quick extravert.

74

grace of line. In his *Annunciation* in the Uffizi this light-footedness is exaggerated into positive instability. The Renaissance pictures of the Virgin afford an infinite number of examples of this ecstatic treatment; the *Sistine Madonna* is a classic one. Among artists El Greco is an extreme type: there is hardly one of his pictures that includes a standing full-length figure which does not exemplify this contradiction of gravity. However different in style, many of Murillo's pictures — for example the various *Immaculate Conceptions* — follow the same scheme. Another such artist is William Blake. Of him Laurence Binyon writes:[1] 'He excels all European artists in one respect: he can make his figures float and rush in air as if that were their native element . . . They float and fly as we imagine ourselves in dreams to be able to do'. Like El Greco, he painted hardly a picture in which at least one figure is not contradicting gravity. In adopting this scheme the quick extravert artist unconsciously emphasizes his contempt of natural law, by portraying a supernatural world that is beyond law. In religious art such compositions have a certain intellectual justification;[2] but they become wholly factitious when the painter applies them to other themes and portrays lovely ladies in unnaturally floating drapery walking with unearthly lightness.[3] Even the seated figure of Madame de Pompadour by Boucher[4] shows the same want of weight and balance; and certain street-scenes by Utrillo suggest the application of the levita-

---

[1] p. 179. This floating effect is sometimes found in drawings by hysteric patients. See for example H. PRINZHORN, *Bildnerei der Geisteskranken*, 2nd ed. Berlin, 1923, p. 187, and M. Réja, *L'Art chez les fons*, n. d.

[2] But hardly when Cosimo Tura destroys the traditional dignity of the Child in the Virgin's arms.

[3] Gainsborough used this attitude even for his portraits of men; e.g. the early *David Garrick* now at Stratford on Avon.

[4] Baron M. de Rothschild's collection.

tional scheme to landscape, as do certain still-lifes by Picasso, Monet and Van Gogh to inanimate objects.[1] This denial of gravity may even find sculptural expression, but only by artists of superb technique and infinite audacity. Bernini's *Apollo and Daphne*[2] and his *Ecstatic Vision of St. Theresa*[3] are both denials of weight translated into stone.

This same reluctance to be bound by obvious natural law sometimes finds a subtler expression in compositions made from so unusual an angle that the commonplace perspective is avoided. The scheme may be found as early as the fifteenth century, in such pictures as Stefano da Verona's *Madonna and Child with St. Catherine in a rose garden.*[4] Tintoretto characteristically uses it in his *Last Supper* painted for San Giorgio Maggiore at Venice in 1594. It finds its fullest expression, however, in the work of such modern painters as Claude Monet. His *Boulevard des Capucines au Carnaval* and *Intérieur après dîner* are both taken from a height sufficient to give a strange aspect to familiar things,[5] and his paintings of pools of water-lilies are made from angles that transport us into a fairy world. The unusual point of view adds something which may be compared with the mystical experiences sometimes associated with the sight of a landscape from an unusual angle.[6]

In compositions in which a normal perspective and stability are followed the quick extravert's dissatisfaction with the world as it is finds expression in a peculiar

---

[1] Another instance is WILLIAM ROBERTS's *Brass Balls* illustrated in WILENSKI, *Modern Movement in Art*, Plate 19.

[2] In the Borghese Gallery, Rome.

[3] In the Church of Sta. Maria delle Vittoria at Rome.

[4] In the Verona Gallery.

[5] Cf. Van Gogh's *Washerwoman* (in the Hamburg Museum) and his *Café de Nuit*.

[6] Cf. W. JAMES, *The Varieties of Religious Experience*, 1902, p. 70 and p. 395.

confusion and urgency of line. Worringer writes of German Gothic art:[1] 'The unsatisfied impulse existing in this confusion of lines, clutching greedily at every new intensification, to lose itself finally in the infinite, is its impulse, its life. It is this exalted hysteria which is above all else the distinguishing mark of the Gothic phenomenon'. The quality is certainly evident in many of the late-medieval German paintings that Worringer illustrates: for instance, the *Crucifixion* in the Church of St. Stephen at Mainz, the *Entombment* of the Church of St. James at Göttingen and the *Crown of Thorns* in the Regler Kirche at Erfurt; and in such sculpture as Riemenschneider's altarpiece in the Church of St. Peter and St. Paul at Heidelberg. The quality is much less often evident in the medieval art of France: an exceptional instance is the tympanum of the great door of Vézelay.

The quick extravert is apt to set colour above form — El Greco declared that 'el colorido es superior al dibujo' — and is less shocked by his own drawing than men of other temperaments often are. His aim is

To bring the invisible full into play!
Let the visible go to the dogs — what matters?

Because of this emphasis on colour, and because his rejection of the laws of gravity is with difficulty reconcilable with plastic necessities, the quick extravert is less often a sculptor than a painter. When he is, he achieves in place of colour a sculptural *morbidezza*. This will be found in works as distant in time as the Hermes of Praxiteles, the head of Sainte Fortunade from the Corrèze and the work of Sir Alfred Gilbert. An extreme instance is the sculpture of Medardo Rosso.

[1] *Form in Gothic* (trans. H. Read) 1927. UHDE (*Picasso et la tradition française*) also stresses this transcendental quality, and finds it underlying the Greek, Spanish, and German Genius.

77

The quick extravert is not naturally attracted to landscape, unless it be as the background of a *Fête galante*.[1] On the rare occasions when he paints pure landscape, it would seem as if he strove to find in it the expression of a personal sentiment rather than the disinterested emotion which inspires the quick introvert. Van Gogh writes to his brother:

'A row of pollarded willows sometimes resembles a procession of almshouse men. Young corn has something inexpressibly pure and tender about it which awakens the same emotion as the expression of a sleeping baby . . . A few days ago, when it had been snowing, I saw a group of white cabbages standing frozen and benumbed, that reminded me of a group of women in their thin petticoats and old shawls which I had seen early in the morning standing near a coffee stall.'[2] Later, when it was a question not of seeing but of painting a picture, the same sentimental preoccupation continues to be evident:[3]

'I have a view of the Rhône — the iron bridge at Trinquetaille — in which sky and river are the colour of absinthe, the quays a shade of lilac, the figures leaning on the parapet blackish, the iron bridge an intense blue, with a note of vivid orange in the background and a note of intense malachite . . . I am trying to get something utterly heart-broken.' Not thus would Cotman or Turner have written. A certain instability of composition is evident even in the landscapes of the quick extraverts. Laurence Binyon has pointed out[4] that Fire is Blake's

[1] Cf. C. F. PERRIOLLAT, *Le Surnaturel dans l'Art*, 1927, p. 34. 'L'art du paysage a été longtemps maintenu au second plan; c'est en effet sa vraie place et son vrai rôle . . . Assez de cet art facile qui n'est qu'un pis aller pour les incapables et les paresseux!'
[2] *Letters of Vincent Van Gogh to his Brother*, II, 12.
[3] Quoted DEWEY, *Art as Experience*, 1934, p. 85. The intensity and variety of his religious experience likewise suggests the diagnosis of a quick extravert.
[4] p. 179.

most constant subject: 'the flames which rush up and leap and bend and flicker' — and there is a flamelike quality about Van Gogh's paintings of flowers and even of landscape — for example, *Le Ravin* and *The Cypress Tree*[1] — that is another expression of this tendency.[2]

In decoration, as in other art, the quick extravert loves to deny the sense of gravity; a remarkable instance is that column from the Abbaye de Coulombs[3] in which traditional architectural forms and ornament in stone are not only twisted as if they had been cast in clay and contorted in a plastic state, but are also broken by human figures that seem to swim and float on the violent stream of ornament.

As in his landscape, there is often a flamelike instability about a quick extravert's schemes of decoration. Normally such ornament is confined to its native boudoir; occasionally it makes an appearance in other fields. Those who are not quick extraverts and know Gaudi's Portal of the Nativity in the church of the Sagrada Familia at Barcelona, will have readily believed the rumour that it was one of the first ecclesiastical buildings to be attacked by the mob at the outbreak of the Civil War.

Architecture is, in the main, an art too strictly immobilized and too straitly conditioned by stability for the quick extravert;[4] but certain styles, in their reduction of pure structure to a *chassis* for scenic effects, suggest the quick extravert mind. Such are those Italian churches

[1] In the Tate Gallery.
[2] On flame symbolism in the religious imagery of hysteria see JANET, *De l'angoisse à l'extase*, 1926-28, I, p. 118.
[3] Now in the Louvre.
[4] Certain appreciations of buildings by men of this temperament are remarkable for their stress on instability. Procopius, describing Santa Sophia rebuilt after its destruction in 532, describes the pillars of the apse as set like dancers in a chorus; likens the great piers to precipitous cliffs, and says that the dome seems to hang by a golden thread from Heaven.

that are all façade and interior, with barn-like exterior sides that are not meant to be seen. Such too are those rococo structures in which everything is made subservient to ornament and every line is curved in at least three directions; and such are the productions of the 'art Nouveau' of the 1900's, with a fluidity and softness of line that recalls the quality that Verlaine demands for poetry:

> De la musique avant toute chose;
> Et pour cela préfère l'Impair
> Plus vague et plus soluble dans l'air
> Sans rien en lui qui pèse ou qui pose.

A very curious example of such architecture was the *Goetheanum* built by the 'anthroposophical' followers of Steiner. Their gospel was a farrago of mysticism derived from many sources; and their temple was its perfect architectural expression.[1]

IV

The quick introvert is often versatile enough to work in more than one field, but two *genres* are peculiarly his: decoration and landscape. As a decorator he is generally anonymous; but in all the field of ornament that is based on natural forms, from Minoan pots through Greek gems and Gothic sculpture and illumination to Turkish brocades and Audenarde tapestries, we may recognize his hand. He loves the sweetness of a curve more than the rigidity of geometric forms; but his

[1] R. STEINER, *Ways to a new style in Architecture*, 1917 (Lectures mostly given about 1914) and A. ROSENKRANTZ, *The Goetheanum as a new impulse in Art*, n.d. (1934). The Goetheanum was unfortunately destroyed by fire in 1921; I have not seen its successor.

designs have a boldness of idea, a consistency of form, that makes them completely different from the soft and graceful achievements of the quick extravert. Similarly, his colours run through a deeper and more resonant gamut than the quick extravert's pale and elegant hues; but blacks and whites he usually eschews, preferring dark browns and creamy yellows for his extreme tints. His decoration is often sculptured, but it has always the curve of natural growth rather than the angularity of stone, whether it be the plane leaves that lie upon the surface of a Roman altar, the budding foliage of a Gothic capital, or the more formal leafage of Donatello's balustrade. Even in iron work it will lose all spear-like quality and be as easy and gracious in its curves as is the gate of the Casa de Pilatos at Seville. Something so formal as script he will turn from Trajanic severity into a decorative arabesque, whether it be the Gothic alphabet of the Studley Royal bowl[1] or the magnificent Cufic of such metal-work as Alp Arslan's silver dish and of such architectural ornament as that of the Mosque of Sultan Hassan.

The quick introvert decorator enjoys many of the forms of classical architecture, but is apt to use them freely and unclassically, as decoration rather than as architecture. At its worst his enjoyment of curves and mouldings for their own sake may become as extravagant as the interior of the Cartuja at Granada; at its best it may have the sober dignity and elegant proportion of Philibert de l'Orme's 'French Order' or of the French classicism of Versailles. It is never very scholarly; and the classic purity of line is often obscured. We may suspect his hand in the most diverse buildings in which architecture and ornament are completely fused, whether in the

[1] In the Victoria and Albert Museum.

Erechtheum at Athens, or in the Mosque of the Dome of the Rock at Jerusalem, or in Exeter Cathedral or in the cloister at Gloucester. Such work will often show two characteristics: a preference for the ogival line, and a multiplication of structural forms in order to achieve decorative effect. The ogival line will be found in structures as diverse as the Alhambra at Granada, the Lady Chapel at Ely, the tower of Jacques Cœur's house at Bourges, the choir screen at Albi and the baroque baldacchino of the Cathedral of Worms. The multiplication of forms recurs as far apart in time and space as the Alhambra of Granada and Tessin's Riddarhus at Stockholm. We are apt to accept all Gothic as structural; but Exeter Cathedral might well have been built with fewer than sixteen colonnettes to the piers, eightfold mouldings to the archivolts and eleven ribs to the vaulting.

I have already instanced William Morris as a quick introvert. He may stand as the type of all the unnamed decorators and architects of that temperament. Characteristically plenteous in production[1] and generous in mind; impulsive, yet with a deep-lying consistency of purpose, hot tempered, self-centred, decisive; in everything responsive to beauty and in everything a reformer. His biographer tells us: 'To him the House Beautiful represented the visible form of life itself. Not only as a craftsman and manufacturer, a worker in dyed stuffs and textiles and glass, a pattern designer and decorator, but throughout the whole range of life, he was from first to

[1] 'It may give some idea of the prodigious mass of his work as a designer to add that the sum total of his designs for paper hangings, chintzes, woven stuffs, silk damasks, stamped velvets, carpets and tapestries (excluding the hand-made carpets and Arras tapestries, which were each specially designed and as a rule not duplicated) which were actually carried out, amounts to little short of six hundred, besides countless designs for embroidery.' MACKAIL, Life of William Morris, II, 57.

last the architect, the master-craftsman, whose range of work was so phenomenal and his sudden transitions from one to another form of productive energy so swift and perplexing because, himself secure in the centre, he struck outwards to any point on the circumference with equal directness, with equal precision, unperplexed by artificial subdivisions of art, and untrammelled by any limiting rules of professional custom.'[1] It is entirely characteristic that he considered the qualities fatal to art to be vagueness, hypocrisy and cowardice.[2]

In his pictures and sculpture as in his designs the quick introvert has always a strong sense of weight.[3] Compare with a Byzantine mosaic a painting by Mantegna, that has a massiveness that gives to his figures what we call a sculptural quality, since material weight is inescapably bound up with plastic art. Compare with the levitational scheme of the Sistine Madonna the triptych of the *Virgin Enthroned* by the Maître de Moulins. She sits in an aureole nimbed by a glory of rainbow light, and beyond it floats a circle of adoring angels. Yet the Virgin and the angels alike obey the laws of gravity, and their earthly weight in no wise detracts from their heavenly beauty. Compare with the weight of a figure painted by Gainsborough the weight of a figure painted by Reynolds, and the same contrast is evident; one tends to float, the other stands.

A quick introvert's compositions tend to be static; it is not that his personages cannot move, but they are not moving at the moment when he portrays them. Compare the dynamic schemes of Rodin with the static

[1] MACKAIL, op. cit., I, 78. [2] Ibid., II, 20.
[3] Cf. HUME, *Treatise on Human Nature*, Bk. II, Pt. II, sect. 5. 'There is no rule in painting more reasonable than that of ballancing the figures, and placing them with the greatest exactness on their proper center of gravity. A figure, which is not justly ballanc'd, is disagreeable; and that because it conveys the idea of its fall, of harm, and of pain.'

compositions of his pupil Maillol, and you see the difference between extravert and introvert sculpture. No sculptor can lay less stress on muscle than Maillol, or more on static mass. Bronzino balances the traditional dynamic scheme of his *Christ in Limbo* by the static figure of a woman, just as Manet stresses and centres his *Musique aux Tuileries* with the static seated figures in the left foreground. Even when the figures are in motion they still obey the laws of gravity; Mantegna's dancing figures in *Parnassus* have more weight than Botticelli's standing ones.[1] The quick introverts' are the compositions which Mademoiselle Marcelle Wahl[2] has qualified as 'immobilized'. A quick introvert artist most often finds religious significance in a scheme of hieratic stability; Berenson admirably defines this quality as 'processional gravity'.

The quick introvert's innate gift for simplification — 'the liberating of what is significant from what is not'[3] — makes him paint pictures that are stylized designs, interpretations of nature far more vivid than any exacter portrayals. Wilson's *Snowdon*, for example, is no topographical study,[4] nor does it slavishly follow the classical tradition of Italian landscape, yet few pictures better convey the essential beauty of the landscape of Wales. In these compositions there is often a great sense of

[1] Cf. VERNON LEE and C. A. Thompson, *Beauty and Ugliness*, p. 307. 'Botticelli . . . has an odd intermittence in his pattern and in his energy. You expect a given sort of line – say the other side of an ogive, which he prepares you for by small indications. But he suspends the fulfilment by a brusque line – say a vertical . . . With Leonardo the intricacy is always a mere unexpected *more*, an increase of complexity in harmony. The one sort of temperament might lead to religious mania, the other be associated very naturally with the passion for nature and generalization.'

[2] *Le mouvement dans la peinture*, 1936.

[3] CLIVE BELL, *Art*, p. 12.

[4] '[Turner] had a horror of what he said Wilson called "being too mappy".' THORNBURY, *Life of J. M. W. Turner, R.A.*, 1877, p. 104. 'Peintre d'histoire' was the worst insult Manet could offer to an artist. E. MOREAU NÉLATON, *Manet raconté par lui-même*, 1926, I, p. 21.

space and distance caused by crossing and receding planes;[1] and often a sense of what Morris calls 'the melancholy born of beauty'. For if the slow extravert brings wit into art, and the quick gaiety, the art of the introvert is always serious. Roger Fry[2] has left a remarkable description of the process by which such a composition is achieved:

'Almost any turn of the kaleidoscope of nature may set up in the artist a detached and aesthetic vision, and, as he contemplates the particular field of vision, the (aesthetically) chaotic and accidental contemplation of forms and colours begins to crystallize into a harmony; and, as this harmony becomes clear to the artist, his actual vision becomes distorted by the emphasis of the rhythm that is set up within him. Certain relations of line become for him full of meaning; he apprehends them no longer curiously but passionately, and these lines begin to be so stressed and stand out so clearly from the rest that he sees them more distinctly than he did at first. Similarly, colours which in nature have almost always a certain vagueness and elusiveness, become so definite and clear to him, owing to their now so necessary relation to other colours, that, if he chooses to paint his vision, he can state it positively and definitely.'[3] As Binyon[4] says of Francis Towne, 'His attitude, perhaps, is intellectual even more than emotional. He feels the need to understand.' This is confirmed by some of the

[1] Is it more than a verbal coincidence that Mackail speaks of the 'receding planes of action ... interlaced or interfused' of Morris's *Love is Enough?* Op. cit., I, p. 281.
[2] Quoted DEWEY, p. 86.
[3] Cf. William Morris: 'I had three very good days at Kelmscott: once or twice I had that delightful quickening of perception by which everything gets emphasized and heightened, and the commonest landscape looks lovely.' Quoted MACKAIL, *Life of William Morris*, II, p. 187.
[4] Op. cit., p. 89. He is speaking of Towne's *Mountains* in the Victoria and Albert Museum.

precepts in Leonardo da Vinci's[1] treatise on painting. All our knowledge, he says, comes from feeling; but the painter should always be transmuting into thought the things that he sees and always be conscious of the effect of their surroundings upon their light and colour. He sets painting before sculpture because it is inimitable; and characteristically combines the need for a fine theory to precede practice with a need for the direct and profound observation of nature. This same need for the transmutation of things seen by thought has been likewise felt by quick introverts whose medium is words: Keats writes of 'the innumerable compositions and decompositions which take place between the intellect and its thousand materials before it arrives at that trembling, delicate and snail-horn perception of beauty'.[2] So Shelley saw the artist in his *Prometheus Unbound*:

> He will watch from dawn to gloom
> The lake-reflected sun illume
> The yellow bees in the ivy bloom,
> Nor heed nor see what things they be;
> But from these create he can
> Forms more real than living man,
> Nurselings of immortality.

This intellectual force may make it hard for the quick introvert artist to devote himself entirely to his art,[3] but it will lead him to attempt new and modern subjects. It is Turner who first makes a railway train[4] and a

---

[1] I do not accept FREUD's *Leonardo da Vinci* (1910) as art criticism; but even he considers Leonardo da Vinci as of manic type.

[2] Quoted JOHN DEWEY, *Art as Experience*, 1934, p. 70.

[3] Cf. C. J. HOLMES, *Leonardo da Vinci* (Henriette Hertz Lecture, British Academy), 1919, p. 4: 'Like a steady refrain through all [his] story there runs the record of absorption in scientific enquiries, by which his achievements in art were constantly delayed, left unfinished, or damaged irretrievably'.

[4] *The Great Western Railway* (National Gallery). About 1871 Manet even painted a picture of a man on a bicycle.

steamer[1] the centres of pictures in which the actual facts are transmuted into a strange beauty that is yet essentially true.

The quick introvert's need for simplification of scheme is sometimes, especially outside landscape, balanced by his delight in decorative detail.[2] Mantegna paints an *Adoration* in which one of the Kings from the East offers the Child a bowl of blue and white Persian porcelain; Domenico Ghirlandajo delights in jewels; Bartolommeo Veneto uses them almost as a signature, and Simone Martini combines a characteristic emphasis on formal line, balance and weight with exquisite flower detail, delicately figured brocade, jewelled ornament, and elaborate woodwork, in a fashion that shows that had he not been a great painter he would have been a great decorative artist.

It is comparatively rarely that a quick introvert devotes himself to portraiture. When he does the picture is transmuted into something essentially decorative. The well-known portraits of the Duke and Duchess of Montefeltro by Piero della Francesca may stand as examples:[3] characterized yet stylized, perfectly static, exquisite in their decorative detail, and set against a landscape background, only a quick introvert could have painted them. The same characteristics reappear in the Renaissance in Bronzino; and their essentials will be found in work as apparently diverse as the portraits of Reynolds and Manet.

The quick introvert artist is apt to travel by other roads than the main highway of the art of his day. He is apt to have far more in common with quick introverts of

---

[1] *The Fighting Témeraire* and *Burial at Sea of Sir David Wilkie*.

[2] Cf. HAVELOCK ELLIS, *A Study of British Genius*, 1927, p. 220: 'The Celtic poet's . . . method is always *decorative* . . . he is always concerned to find the beautiful and harmonious details'.

[3] The profile is often chosen by the quick introvert portrait painter, probably because it lends itself to a decorative composition.

other periods than with his own contemporaries. With all their differences of date and style there is an obvious fellowship between Claude Lorrain, Richard Wilson, Francis Towne, Cotman, Turner, Sisley and C. J. Holmes: a community of temperament hard to express in words, but easily felt, especially by those who share that temperament, however inexpressively. Often the quick introverts have to be content, like Cotman,[1] to paint masterpieces that satisfy their own tastes, though no one else of their generation appreciates them. But after a century or more some critic may arise to describe their work as sympathetically as Binyon has described Cotman's *Greta Bridge*.[2]

'All the elements of the scene; the large rocks in the water; the woods, the building in the middle distance, the clouds along the sky; all these are harmonized and brought into intimate relations with each other, while the light in the sky and the clear reflections of it in the water enliven and enhance the more solid masses. Everything has been transformed in the mind of the artist, with its instinctive search for rhythmical relations. And yet there is no forcing or distortion of nature . . . but . . . a perfect balance between natural form and the preconceived design.'

Unfortunately the quick introvert artist's dependence on social life and his peculiar sense of his audience may easily lead him away from his own especial field. Turner[3]

---

[1] 1782-1842. Wilenski suggests that he was a manic depressive. *English Painting*, 1933, p. 209.
[2] Op. cit., p. 124.
[3] Ruskin's description of his characteristics sums up the manic temperament: 'Uprightness, generosity, tenderness of heart (extreme), sensuality, obstinacy (extreme), irritability, infidelity. And be sure that he knew his own power, and felt himself utterly alone in the world from its not being understood'. W. THORNBURY, *The Life of J. M. W. Turner, R.A.*, 1877, p. xi. He was in his own line as prolific as Morris, and left hundreds of sketch books and twenty thousand sketches. Ibid., xii.

tried to paint in the style of Italian and French and Dutch masters, to be a conventionally classical artist, before he learned to be himself. Corot, who was essentially a quick introvert, advised 'Never paint a subject unless it calls insistently and directly upon your eye and heart';[1] but the demands of his day caused him to produce many pictures that are not characteristically his. His Salon nudes, his figures with Poussinesque grey flesh, his classical landscapes, his woolly trees, have no permanent individual value. But in certain landscapes wherein the changing beauties of provincial France will last for ever — in the *Maisons sur les quais à Honfleur*,[2] *La Seine à Rouen, Villefranche lès Avignon* — and in some of the Roman pictures, the man is painting with absolute sincerity in complete accord with his innate ideal of beauty.[3]

V

Fuseli[4] distinguished three *genres* of painting: 'the epic or sublime, the dramatic or impassioned, and the historic or circumscribed by truth; the first astonishes, the second moves, the third informs'. The three types of slow extravert art could not be more clearly differentiated. To each the slow extravert artist brings a characteristic touch of megalomania. *Le style noble* is his: those immense *Descents from the Cross* of Titian and Rubens, those *Last Judgements* of Michelangelo, those morbid *Entombments* and sensual *Magdalenes*. His, too, is usually the most brilliant technique: there is a conscious *bravura* about

---

[1] Quoted MRS. LAURENCE BINYON, *The Mind of the Artist*, 1909, p. 38.
[2] Exhibited at the French gallery in 1926.
[3] Similarly Edward Lear shows himself a true quick introvert artist in his sketches, and merely an accomplished Victorian painter in his finished work.
[4] 'A History of Art in the Schools of Italy' in *Life and Works*, ed. J. Knowles, 1931, II, 156.

Hals' *Cavalier*, Rubens's *Helène Fourment* and Hogarth's *Shrimp Girl* which is characteristic. It is often counterbalanced by a lack of capacity for finding new ideas for artistic expression; no artist is so conservative in his themes, or so dependent on the 'donneurs d'idées' of his day for subjects.[1] Fromentin declares[2] 'il s'écoula près d'un siècle pendant lequel la grande école hollandaise parut ne plus penser à rien qu'à bien peindre'. This was the century after the Reformation had destroyed the code of Catholic iconography, within which the slow extravert painter could find themes suited to his skill.

If the quick extravert tends to the levitational in his schemes, and the quick introvert to the static, the slow extravert's bent is towards the dynamic. I have already written of that doctrine of empathy by which the slow extravert seeks to explain his muscular sympathy with what he sees portrayed before him. This feeling, consciously or not, determines not only the compositions of the slow extravert but also to some extent his subjects. 'To realize the play of muscles everywhere, to get the full sense of the various pressures and resistances, to receive the direct inspiration of the energy expended, we must have the nude; for here alone can we watch those tautnesses of muscle and those stretchings and relaxings and ripplings of skin which, translated into similar strains in our own person, make us fully realize movement.'[3]

We have material enough from Vasari[4] to establish the fact that Michelangelo was of slow extravert tempera-

---

[1] L. MARCH PHILLIPPS, writing in 1911, said 'modern art . . . can paint or carve anything it likes exactly in the manner it likes; at the same time it does not know in the least what to paint or carve'. He puts it down to the Pre-Raphaelites who broke up 'authority and law and let loose upon us the whole flood of hitherto controlled and organized dexterity'. *The Works of Man*, p. 266.

[2] *Les Maîtres d'Autrefois* (1910 ed., p. 181).

[3] B. BERENSON, *Florentine Painters of the Renaissance*, p. 86.

[4] *Lives of the most eminent painters and sculptors*, trans. G. du C. de Vere, 1912-15, IX, p. 11 *et seq.*, 105 *et seq.*

ment. He 'delighted in solitude', we are told; 'although he was rich, he lived like a poor man, nor did any friend ever eat at his table, or rarely; and he would not accept presents from anyone, because it appeared to him that if anyone gave him something, he would be bound to him for ever'. At times he came near to megalomania. He went to Carrara to see about marble for the tomb of Pope Julius. 'There, in those mountains, he spent eight months without other moneys or supplies; and he had many fantastic ideas of carving great statues in those quarries, in order to leave memorials of himself as the ancients had done before him.' Characteristically, too, he retired in old age into a somewhat squalid solitude.

He may stand as a type of the slow extravert in his dynamic compositions, his preference for sculpture over painting, and his glorification of the magnified human body; magnified not only in scale, but also in power and importance. The Sistine Chapel, with its sculpturally treated human figures in movement against a rigidly angular architectural frame, is typical of the slow extravert. 'See how he divides that ceiling in such a way that the frames of the separate compositions combine into a huge structure of painted rafters and brackets, nay the Prophets and Sibyls, the Ancestors and Ancestresses themselves, and the naked antique genii, turn into architectural members, holding that imaginary roof together, securing its seeming stability, increasing by their gesture its upspring and its weightiness, and at the same time determining the tracks along which the eye is forced to travel. Backwards and forwards the eye is driven by this living architecture, round and round in its search now for completion of visible pattern, now for symbolic and narrative meaning.'[1] Michelangelo's treatment of

---

[1] VERNON LEE, *The Beautiful*, p. 123.

seated figures — necessarily the most static of subjects — shows how far he was dominated by the idea of a dynamic composition. The *Pietà* in St. Peter's is given dynamic movement by the dramatic treatment of the Virgin's pointing hand and by the swirl of her draperies; and the Libyan Sibyl of the Sistine Frescoes shows his characteristic impatience with the seated pose: she is represented, as Vasari points out, rising and half-turning to shut her prophetic book. Michelangelo is equally true to type in his despisal of the Flemish school, 'who are content to paint hovels, over-green fields shaded by trees, rivers and bridges, what are called *landscapes* . . . in which, though it may in some eyes make a good effect, there is in truth neither art nor reason'.[1]

Equally characteristic are the dynamic compositions of Titian, reaching their climax in the *Gloria* of the Prado, in which the Divine figures are the only ones not in violent movement. Even their repose he did not always respect; witness the violent movement of the Child in the Madonna of the Munich Pinakothek. He even modified the traditional scheme of the Virgin and Child, adored by the donor of the picture and his patron saints. In such a picture in the Church of San Domenico at Ancona the Virgin and Child appear as a vision from the clouds; St. Francis gazes upon them in ecstasy, and his patron saint points out the vision to the donor with a dramatic forefinger. The only important religious composition of Titian's which is not in violent motion is the famous *Presentation*[2] that gains a dramatic effect less from its figures than from its architecture.

---

[1] Quoted E. Michel, *Nouvelles Études sur l'histoire de l'art*, p. 175. The point of view goes back to Aristotle, who did not rank landscapes and animals among the objects of aesthetic imitation. It has found expression even in our own century in A. M. Ludovici, *Nietzsche and Art*, 1911, p. 150, which sets landscape definitely below any painting that concerns itself with man.

[2] In the Accademia at Venice.

Another slow extravert artist is Andrea dal Castagno, of whom Berenson has noted the characteristic 'tendency to communicate at any cost a feeling of power'.[1] Vasari[2] not only describes his qualities in terms that perfectly fit the slow extravert: intelligent in technique, excelling in draughtsmanship but not in colouring, and showing 'very great boldness in the movement of his figures and much vehemence in the heads of men and women', but also completes the picture by describing him as 'that miserable Andrea del Castagno, who was truly great and excellent in painting and design, but even more notable for the rancour and envy that he bore towards other painters'. His dramatic sense found its truest expression in the sternly rectilinear composition of his *Last Supper* in the convent of S. Apollonia at Florence, with only the traitor figure of Judas to break the architectural scheme. The pen-drawings — most characteristic because least technically laboured — of Rembrandt give the effect of a scene of tragedy: Roger Fry rightly says of Rembrandt,[3] 'had he expressed himself in words, he would, one cannot help believing, have been one of the greatest dramatists or novelists that has ever been, whilst his plastic constructions are equally supreme'.

Delacroix — a typical slow extravert — wrote: 'Si je ne suis pas agité comme un serpent dans la main d'une pythonisse, je suis froid'.[4] Mademoiselle Marcelle Wahl[5] has similarly analysed two modes of vision in such artists: one by mass, with the composition conceived in

---

[1] *Florentine Painters*, p. 40.   [2] Op. cit., III, p. 97.
[3] *Transformations*: critical and speculative essays on art, 1926, p. 21.
[4] E. MOREAU-NÉLATON, *Delacroix raconté par lui-même*, 1916, I, p. 112.
[5] *Le mouvement dans la peinture*, 1936, p. 112. In her view: 'Toute artiste véritable est habité par deux tendances opposées, expressions de deux mouvements contraires qu'il cherche à équilibrer: le mouvement "immobilisé" . . . et le mouvement "en mouvement", le dynamisme . . . C'est par la prédominance de l'un ou l'autre que se différencient les tempéraments créateurs.'

lines of force, and one by line, with the composition conceived in lines of limitation. If he does not emulate the
dramatic gesticulation of Hellenistic sculpture, the slow
extravert is apt to express his idealism in the chilly
classicism of Canova or Flaxman, David or Ingres. An
extreme instance is Ingres's *Jupiter and Thetis*: cold, life-
less, and inspired by a desire for that classical beauty
which Winckelmann described as being like pure water,
quite tasteless.[1] Ingres, when he declared that he stood
for 'point de couleur trop ardente, c'est anti-historique',
and when he remarked that 'l'art anti-classique, si tant
est que ce soit un art, n'est qu'un art de paresseux',
reduced to words instincts felt by every slow extravert artist who leans rather to classicism than to
drama.

I have already mentioned Titian, Rembrandt, Ingres
and Delacroix among the slow extraverts. Anyone who
recalls such portraits by Titian as that of the *Elector of
Saxony*, such by Rembrandt as the *Portrait of a Rabbi*,[2]
such by Ingres as *M. Bertin* and such by Delacroix as
Henri Hugues, will not need to be told that just as the slow
extravert writer, with his strong sense of fact, is often
gifted in biography, so the painter of the same temperament is often gifted in portraiture. In such pictures
tradition (and a sense of appropriateness) usually forbids
a dynamic scheme: but even so a slow extravert's portraits are generally much less stylized in scheme than
those of a quick introvert. If the people sit still, some
accessory may be in movement; in Rubens's portrait of
the Earl of Arundel and his wife[3] the composition is
dominated by a wind-blown banner.

Rubens is primarily a portrait painter; witness the

---

[1] Quoted G. SÉAILLES, *L'origine et les destinées de l'art*, 1925, p. 76.
[2] Collection of M. Gulbenkian; from the Hermitage.
[3] At Munich.

magnificent portrait of Helène Fourment or her sister that has lately been on view at the National Gallery,[1] and the figure of Marie de Medicis that stands out among 'the explosions of Cupids'[2] of his decorative paintings in the Louvre.[3] Eugène Fromentin has admirably seized the qualities and defects of such portraiture.[4]

'Sont ils ressemblants? Oui, à peu près. Sont ils vivants? Ils vivent, plus qu'ils ne sont . . . le peintre . . . les a regardés à la légère, par l'epiderme, peut-être à travers des habitudes, sans doute à travers une formule. Les drames, les passions, les attitudes des corps, les expressions des visages, c'est-à-dire l'homme entier dans les multiples incidents de la scène humaine, tout cela passe à travers son cerveau, y prend des traits plus forts, des formes plus robustes, s'amplifie, ne s'épure pas, mais se transfigure dans je ne sais quelle apparence héroïque. Il imprime partout la netteté de son caractère, la chaleur de son sang, la solidité de sa stature, l'admirable équilibre de ses nerfs, et la magnificence de ses ordinaires visions.' They have not the compassionate psychology of a portrait by Velasquez; but they have brilliance and competence of their own.

This bent also extends, I think, to satiric portraits and caricatures. It is the slow extravert who puts wit into art, as does the quick extravert gaiety. Delacroix, with his pictures of conflict between beast and beast, man and beast, man and man, must have been of slow extravert

[1] Collection of M. Gulbenkian; from the Hermitage.
[2] The phrase is Constable's, *Letters of John Constable, R.A., to C. R. Leslie, R.A.*, ed. P. Leslie, 1931, p. 183.
[3] Rubens, too, organized his work on a typical extravert basis. 'Once established, he had his fixed price, and the kind of picture he painted depended on the amount he was paid. He did not vary his quality — not consciously — but the size and complication of the picture were strictly determined by the contract.' READ, op. cit., p. 89. See also FROMENTIN, op. cit., p. 132: 'Il estimait ses tableaux à raison de 100 florins par jour'.
[4] *Les maîtres d'autrefois* (1910 ed., pp. 107, 130).

temperament, and it has been pointed out[1] how close his psychological portraits come to caricature. Daumier and Rowlandson were probably slow extraverts, and in their more elaborate compositions show the characteristic dynamic schemes. Daumier's *Gare Saint Lazare* has the same dramatic force as a sketch by Rembrandt. I think it likely, too, that it is the slow extravert artists who in an age dominated by decoration are driven to express themselves in grotesque and monstrous ornament.

In certain examples of the work of slow extravert artists a paranoid sadism is evident.[2] A terrible example is the crucified body of Our Lord in the Isenheim altarpiece by Matthias Grünewald. I have already cited Daumier as a slow extravert, and of him Baudelaire wrote: 'En effet ses dessins sont souvent pleins de sang et de fureur. Massacres, emprisonnements, arrestations, perquisitions, procès, assommades de la police . . . reparaissent à chaque instant.'[3] Another paranoid artist is Goya, who must in all his latter years have been quite insane. Like most slow extraverts, portrait painting was his *métier*; yet even in his pitiless portrayal of the neurotic Osuna family and in his pictures of the Royal House his understanding is not sympathetic or even detached, but specifically cruel. 'On a background which is merely indicated with a few strokes which hardly indicate space, he impales like a butterfly the human type, mostly in a moment of folly or wickedness.'[4]

[1] H. READ, op. cit., p. 123. He was above everything a painter of motion, and characteristically introduced a live squirrel into a still life.

[2] Cf. L. S. MERCIER, *The Picture of Paris*, trans. W. and E. Jackson, 1929, p. 43: 'Just as on our woeful tragedy-stage there is always a King, and the King is always a tyrant, and the dialogue is always of stabbing him, and of robbing him of his crown and of his life, so is painting given over-much to bloody catastrophes and to a gloomy mania for martyrs' tortures, burnings at the stake, and broken and mutilated limbs. Enter any church and you shall see nothing but executioners leisurely torturing patient saints all over the spandrels.'

[3] C. BAUDELAIRE, 'Curiosités esthétiques', in *Œuvres complètes*, 1885, IV, p. 370.

[4] Klinger, quoted E. D. PUFFER, *Psychology of Beauty*, p. 125.

Only in the equestrian portraits of Charles IV of Bourbon and his wife, and in such pictures as those of General Urrutia and Doña Isabel Corbos de Porcel does a kindred quality of spirit inspire him to do sound sane work. His sketches of society show him a mad Rowlandson, adding horror to coarseness. Even the turkey in one of his rare still-lifes is gruesomely dead. His pictures of war and its retribution, of the *Witches' Sabbat*, of *Saturn devouring his children*, and such like horrors, show him completely mad and hideously enjoying every horror and cruelty. The *Saturn* was painted for the walls of his own dining-room.

I have said that the detached work of monumental sculpture is a typical *genre* of the slow extravert. In this, too, the characteristic qualities and types can be seen as clearly as in painting. The dynamic type of composition is indeed even more essentially plastic than pictorial:[1] it is found as early as the fifth century B.C. in such work as the Phigaleian frieze, and reaches its apogee in the Hellenistic period, in such work as the Pergamene altar and the Laocoön. Many sculptors might say as Rodin said: 'Even in my less mobile statues I have always tried to give some hint of movement; I have rarely shown complete immobility. I have always tried to render the inner feelings by the mobility of the muscles.'[2] The portrait, too, finds its great first expression in this *genre*, whether in such Egyptian work as the head of Amenemhet III, characteristically carved in hard and refractory obsidian, or in the portrait sculpture of Hellenistic and Roman art.

Just as the quick extravert artist paints 'transcen-

---

[1] It was undoubtedly this quality which made Rubens say: 'I am convinced that to reach the highest degree of perfection as a painter, it is necessary, not only to be acquainted with the ancient statues, but we must be inwardly imbued with a thorough comprehension of them'. MRS. LAURENCE BINYON, *The Mind of the Artist*, 1909, p. 28.

[2] A. RODIN, *L'Art*, Entretiens réunis par P. Gsell, 1911, p. 72.

dental' pictures for men of his own temperament, so does the slow extravert work at 'descriptive' paintings for men of his own kind: paintings which Professor Samuel Alexander fitly compares with prose.[1] To this category belong all those paintings of military, tavern and bourgeois life that are of greater value to the student of social history than to the historian of art. Terborch, Jan Steen, Adriaen van Ostade and Hals may stand as examples.[2] The moralistic twist given to the *genre* by Hogarth in no wise changed its essential character. Frith's *Railway Station* is a perfect example of the type. A man of any temperament may enjoy it as a piece of literature or a document of social history, but only slow extraverts have ever considered it a work of art.

Landscape in the true sense is not for the slow extravert; but he may well be a competent topographical artist, viewing nature, in Constable's words, 'minutely and *cunningly*, but with no greatness or breadth'.[3]

Constable's own *Study of an Elm*[4] is painted with exactly this topographical vision; but like other slow extraverts, he was master of two styles, and his sepia sketch *On the Stour*[5] with no colour and relatively few brush strokes gives all the intensity of dramatic movement. He and Ruysdael, indeed, can both be great landscape painters; but they are great because they can convey the same sense of drama and the same dynamic stress in their clouds and woods and torrents as other painters

[1] *Beauty and Other Forms of Value*, 1933, pp. 17, 106, 109.
[2] See FROMENTIN, op. cit., p. 162. 'La peinture hollandaise . . . ne fut et ne pouvait être que le portrait de la Hollande, son image extérieure, fidèle, exacte, complète, ressemblante, sans nul embellissement. Le portrait des hommes et des lieux, des mœurs bourgeoises, des places, des rues, des campagnes, de la mer, et du ciel, tel devait être, réduit à ses éléments primitifs, le programme suivi par l'école hollandaise, et tel il fut depuis le premier jour jusqu'à son déclin.'
[3] C. R. LESLIE, *Memoirs of the life of John Constable*, 2nd ed., 1845, p. 18.
[4] In the Victoria and Albert Museum.
[5] In the same collection.

convey by their figures. At their calmest their paintings depict the morning after a storm:

> Rent is the fleecy Mantle of the Sky;
> The Clouds fly different; and the sudden Sun,
> By Fits effulgent, gilds the illumined Field,
> And black by Fits the Shadows sweep along,
> A gaily chequered, heart-expanding View.[1]

Exceptionally, too, the slow extravert may find in some inanimate subject something congenial to his temperament. Flaubert writes: 'Je me souviens d'avoir eu des battements de cœur, d'avoir ressenti un plaisir violent en contemplant un mur de l'Acropole, un mur tout nu ... Dans la précision des assemblages, la rareté des éléments, le poli de la surface, l'harmonie de l'ensemble, n'y a-t-il pas une vertu intrinsèque, une espèce de force divine, quelque chose d'éternel comme un principe?'[2] Just thus was Piranesi able to give to his compositions of ruined architecture the same dynamic force and dramatic power that other slow extraverts have given to their personages. No one not of this temperament could have got the same dramatic impression out of a rusticated buttressed wall as he did in his *Foundations of the Mausoleum of Hadrian*. And his temperament found yet more vivid expression in the *Carceri* with their obsessions of staircases and tortures, and their feeling for pure utilitarian structure. They are classical nightmares that are premonitions of modern factories.

I have said that the slow extravert seeks the ideal and the absolute in order to escape from too manifold a world. Sometimes, however, he does not attempt this, but instead plunges into an equally characteristic amplifica-

---

[1] THOMSON, *Autumn* (1730).
[2] Quoted GUYAU, *L'Art au point de vue sociologique*, p. 59.

tion. 'Just as in one direction, starting from the actual, we can reach an abstraction which is the ideal type of all actuality, so in the opposite direction we can reach a type which is the denial of all reality — an inverse ideality, a nightmare of extremes, of all possible distortions that can be imagined on the basis of actuality. The tendency of pictures of this kind is to become merely anecdotic or encyclopedic, and Breughel as a matter of fact did paint pictures which gathered together on one canvas a collection of popular legends or proverbs.'[1] Another critic[2] has pointed out how deeply Breughel was influenced by Alva's persecutions, and how important an element of historical satire they brought into his work.

The slow extravert instincts find a noble expression in architecture. In classical style such men are nearer to Rome than to Greece; the Colosseum is theirs rather than the Parthenon, St. Peter's at Rome rather than the Baptistery at Florence. A medieval instance of a slow extravert style is, I think, English Perpendicular architecture: rectilinear, stylized, and extraordinarily consistent to type. The guilds of wealthy merchants who built Long Melford and Lavenham, Blythborough and Southwold (and how many more), had their architecture as well organized as their businesses, and, except for the traditional angel roofs, as devoid of imagination. It is noteworthy how far the decorators in this perpendicular style succeeded in modifying the essential curves of Gothic architecture. In the Divinity School at Oxford, the ogival arch has been reduced to triangular form; on the tower of St. Martin's at Clamecy the emphasis is entirely vertical. With the Renaissance this emphasis on

[1] READ, op. cit., p. 87.
[2] R. H. WILENSKI, An Introduction to Dutch Art, 1929, p. 29.

angular line was finally freed from Gothic influences: the interior of the Capella Medicea at Florence shows how rectangular sixteenth-century decoration could be.

I have already spoken of the Escorial; another instance of slow extravert architecture is Brunelleschi's exterior of the Pitti Palace, severe, great, unadorned save for a practical balustrade and the rustication that increases its effect of austerity. Such buildings arise under despots whose sense of power is unlimited. The same feeling reappears in Napoleonic France, when Chalgrin, the architect of the Arc de Triomphe, considered size an essential of beauty; another clause in the slow extravert's *credo* of art.

The highly organized conditions of modern city life have recently given the slow extraverts fresh fields to conquer. Reinforced concrete is an ideal material for their use; and the modern skyscraper and the modern block of flats, plain as a box and huge as a cliff, are their creations.

In decoration, however, their code is nearly always negative. Like Sir John Soane, they sweep away the commonplaces of classical decoration,[1] and like him find nothing but a few meagre geometric forms to take its place. If they achieve more positive results, it is by turning decoration into another *genre*, and getting the justification for their designs from the aptness of their associations or the closeness of their imitations. It is the slow extravert decorator who designs allusive ornament, like the brocades and *toiles de jouy* with the laurel and oak, eagle and star, NN and medals of the Legion of Honour that were produced in honour of Napoleon, or the furniture with Egyptian decoration that commemorated his Egyptian campaign. It is he who introduces topography

[1] See JOAN EVANS, *Pattern*, 1931, II, p. 128.

into decoration, as in the chintz printed about 1830 with designs of Lime Street Station, Liverpool, with a border portraying the entrance to Euston. It is he, too, who imitates metal in pottery, silk in wallpaper, embroidery in textiles, and the processes of hand-work by machinery. It is he who consciously uses forms as if by their associations they became words, to build up a sentence and express an idea. A man called Dresser in 1873 produced a design[1] of which he said that in it 'I have sought to embody chiefly the one idea of power, energy, force or vigour; and in order to do this I have employed such lines as we see in the bursting buds of spring . . . I have also availed myself of those forms to be seen in certain bones of birds which are associated with the organs of flight . . . as well as those observable in the powerful propelling fins of fish.' It is the slow extravert who ends by organizing decoration into industrial art, and proudly says 'ornament is now as material an interest in a commercial community as . . . any raw material of manufacture whatever'.[2]

VI

The slow introvert artist (at least in the visual arts) is harder to find and to recognize. Hugo van der Goes may stand as an example of pathological intensity.[3] Late in life his natural tendencies became exaggerated, and as a lay brother he suffered so much from religious melancholy that he tried to kill himself. Though the prior tried

[1] *Principles of Decorative Design*, p. 17. The design is illustrated in plate 37.
[2] WORNUM, *The Characteristics of Style*, 1856, p. 6.
[3] See E. DUPRÉ, *Pathologie de l'imagination et de l'émotivité*, 1925, p. 345. 'La mélancolie du peintre Hugo van der Goes'.

to cure him, as David cured Saul, with sweet music, he continued for a long time in a morbid state of self-accusation.

It is therefore fair to take the characteristics of his paintings as typical of a melancholic artist. They prove to be a calmness of colour, an alternation of the range from silver to dark blue and from cream through yellow to brown; and a frontal composition, generally set against a background that runs parallel to the plane of the canvas. This composition is evident both in simple schemes like the *Adam and Eve*,[1] and in complex ones like the *History of Abigail*,[2] and is especially clear in his *Adoration of the Shepherds* in the Uffizi.

These characteristics are equally evident in the work of Vermeer of Delft, using a similar palette to achieve compositions full of quietness and dignity, depending upon tonal relations for their effect.[3] The curiously frontal character of his composition is evident even in a drinking scene like the *Lieb haber* in Dresden,[4] and in a landscape like *Delft from the Rotterdam Canal*.[4] Never has a picture been painted more remorselessly frontal than his *Little Street*.[5] Professor Wilenski has pointed out[6] that his background is always a flat surface and his front often indicated by a curtain, giving a cubic composition. I am inclined to think that this is the type of composition characteristic of the slow introvert, just as a static composition with crossing planes of rhythm is of his quicker brother, and levitational and dynamic schemes of the quick and slow extravert.

---

[1] In the Munich Pinakothek.
[2] Known from a copy in the Musée Royal des arts décoratifs at Brussels.
[3] 'In the case of an interior by Vermeer the formal elements, the relation of lines, proportions, lights and shades, colours, recessions and so on, are the ideal subject of the picture.' R. H. WILENSKI, *Modern Movement in Art*, 1935, p. 35.
[4] At The Hague.   [5] At Amsterdam.
[6] *An Introduction to Dutch Art*, 1929, p. 278.

If this be so, then Velasquez is another slow introvert, for this closed, boxlike composition is characteristic of most of his work.[1] *Las Meniñas* and *Las Hilanderas* are typical examples. His finest portraits are posed against a plain wall; even his mythological pictures, like *Los Borrachos* and *La Fragua de Vulcano*, and his landscapes, like the two views of the Garden of the Villa Medici, are cubically composed. The exceptions to the rule are the less characteristic pictures, *Las Lanzas* and the equestrian and hunting portraits, in which he was following an accepted code. His colouring is equally characteristic, with its emphasis less on colour itself than on the infinite contrast of tone. He is happiest in a picture that ranges from buff to black, with the emphasis on the black, like the full length of the Infante Don Carlos, or from grey to dull brown, as in the small portrait of his wife. When he uses colour he uses it sparingly, as in the pink drapery of *Los Borrachos*. His landscapes are either painted almost in monochrome, like the *View of Saragossa*, or else in the greys and blacks of twilight, like the picture of the garden of Buen Retiro. The same limitation of colour is evident even in his largest pictures: *Las Meniñas* is a composition of grey and blue and black, with flesh tints to relieve it. He painted beneath the glowing skies of Spain, but no strong light invades his work. Rather there is an under-water tone; it is as if the mirror from which he painted had had a greenish tint. In his greater compositions, like *The Lances*, the justice of tone and nobility of line give quality and originality and even grandeur: but they are not his most characteristic work. For in them the interest has shifted from persons to events, and it was persons in whom Velasquez was most acutely interested. He could paint the essential dignity of a human being, even if that

[1] He seems to have used a mirror just as Vermeer did.

being were physically or mentally abnormal: witness his astonishing paintings of dwarfs and fools. He had the slow introvert's power of psychological observation; perhaps if he had lived in our own time he might have been not a painter but a psychiatrist.

Truth of tonal relation, a 'closed' composition, quiet colour and an unforced originality are the marks of the slow introvert artist, but they are more Protean in their manifestations and less easy to recognize than the fantasies of the quick extravert, the megalomania of his slower brother, or the rhythmic schemes of the quick introvert. Yet the slow introvert artist is well worth discovery and study. Such, I think, was that comparatively little known artist Dumesnil de la Tour. Both in *Le Nouveau Né*[1] and in his *St. Sebastian mourned by women*[2] there is the characteristic portrayal of human dignity and the characteristic use of tonal relations to achieve design. Such, too, was Caravaggio, in frontality of composition — witness his *Peter denying Christ* — his emphasis on the plane of the background, his psychological portraits, his stress on tonal values, and above all his austere dignity which sets him apart from most of his Baroque contemporaries.

The typical closed composition, and a typical simple dignity, are evident in certain pictures by Dirk Bouts; his *Annunciation*, formerly in the Hermitage, aptly illustrates the difference of composition existing between paintings by men of this type and those composed by quick introverts and quick and slow extraverts. I think it possible that Jan van Eyck was also of this temperament; his *Virgin of the Carthusian Friar*[3] shows the same feeling after a 'cubical' composition, his portrait of *Marguerite van Eyck*[4] is comparable in its sincerity and simplicity with

[1] In the Museum of Rennes. [2] In the Kaiser Friedrich Museum, Berlin.
[3] Collection of Baron Robert de Rothschild.
[4] In the Bruges Museum.

Velasquez's portrait of his own wife. The same type of composition and the same calmness of feeling characterize Pieter de Hoogh's interiors and Catena's *Saint Jerome*. Of this it has been written,[1] 'We see this picture at once as a whole, as if all the parts of it were connected by invisible ties and obeying an unheard musical beat . . . As a result of double co-ordination, of spatial and temporal relations, we feel as if we were safely enclosed in a haven where the minutes do not seem to pass and the sense of hurry is removed from our lives.'

The most distinguished modern artist whom I would diagnose as a slow introvert is an exception who proves the rule that artists of this temperament are not often landscape painters. Cézanne's pictures are extraordinarily consistent in the use of a 'closed' composition. Just as the quick introvert Sisley paints compositions which almost invariably, by a bridge or stream or road, lead the eye on to a distance, seen or guessed at, so Cézanne's schemes end parallel to the spectator, in sea or ridge or mountain.[2] This closing of the composition is often stressed by a horizontal line — water or wall or plain — at a height of about two-thirds of the breadth. This line recurs in the great majority of the compositions of Seurat: for instance in almost all his landscapes and in such pictures as *La Parade*.

I think a *genre* which has a peculiar attraction for the slow introvert is black-and-white. It is probably significant that Dürer's *Melancholia Generosa* is one of his greatest works;[3] and that his St. Jerome is portrayed in a perfect slow introvert's workroom. The slow introvert's respect

[1] VERNON LEE, *Beauty and Ugliness*, p. 230.
[2] The diagnosis is confirmed by his portraits of his dwarf-friend, Achille Emperaire, that are comparable with the dwarfs of Velasquez, and by the continual emphasis on tonal relations expressed in his letters as in his pictures.
[3] See E. PANOFSKY and F. SAXL. DÜRER'S 'Melancholia I': eine Quellen- und Typen-Geschichtliche Untersuchung. Leipzig — Berlin, 1923.

for craftsmanship, too, seems to be expressed in Dürer's opinion that a fine work of art is well-pleasing to God, and that He 'is angry with such as destroy the works of great mastership, for that is bestowed by God alone'.[1] His diligence, his emphasis on the importance of first principles, his respect for the moral character of the artist, and for the natural bent of the would-be artist, his attempts to find the physical counterparts of the temperamental types, his emphasis on antitheses, and his psychological portraits, even his engraving of a mentally defective peasant,[2] all confirm the diagnosis. But from such a view of him a picture not in his natural vein, such as the *Madonna with the Siskin*,[3] must be excluded.

Architecture, too, is sometimes the slow introvert's field: but his are neither the classical fanes of the slow extravert nor the cathedrals of the quick introvert, but the simple houses in which it is easy to live: especially if a quick introvert help with the interior decoration.

It would seem, then, that each type has not only certain characteristic *genres* but also yet more characteristic types of composition. Both types of introvert have a static composition, the quick marked by receding planes leading the eye to a great distance, and the slow by a box-like composition ending in a plane parallel to the spectator. Both types of extravert have a dynamic composition, the slow, one of muscular energy, and the quick, one of a force that denies the laws of gravity. The quick introvert has a natural bent towards decoration and landscape, the slow towards psychological portraiture. The slow extravert has a natural bent towards classicism and the portrayal of fact in portraits or historical painting; the quick extravert is drawn towards the more unreal

---

[1] W. M. CONWAY, *Literary Remains of Albrecht Dürer*, Cambridge, 1889, p. 153.
[2] *Two peasants at Market*, 1512.
[3] In the Kaiser Friedrich Museum, Berlin.

effects of social life or religious ecstasy. Each man is influenced by his cultural environment and by the demands of the society he serves; yet these natural bents, all the stronger because unconscious, none the less control the very foundations of his work.

CHAPTER V

CONCLUSION

The beautiful object possesses those qualities which bring
the personality into a state of unity and self-completeness
E. D. PUFFER, *The Psychology of*
Beauty, 1905, p. 49

So ends my statement — I cannot call it an investigation
— of the relation between psychological types and the
visual arts. It has not much practical value; the slow
extravert will not furnish his room the better for it, or
the quick introvert keep his the more tidy. The working
artist can be trusted to find the medium that suits him
best, the *genre* that he most loves to paint and the *genre*
that he can sell most easily. The one field in which it
may be of practical value is that of education. The artist
will either work out his own point of view, consciously or
unconsciously, or be a failure; the spectator may be
driven by educational, social or critical influences into
seeing things falsely, and his failure (though just as gross)
will be less evident. It is the duty of every man to discover what works of art he truly admires, and the duty
of every educationist to set him on the right path of
discovery.

'Beauty is no quality in things themselves: it exists
merely in the mind, which contemplates them, and each
mind perceives a different beauty. One person may even
perceive deformity where another is sensible of beauty;
and every individual ought to acquiesce in his own sentiment, without pretending to regulate those of others.' It

is long since Hume wrote this: but not long enough for it to have become a part of educational theory.

If we accept the fact that the natural reaction of each individual mind to the work of art must be respected, as a part of the human personality, and that spontaneity is an essential quality of artistic judgment, the element of compulsion in matters of taste must disappear from the teaching of the history of art, and from that dangerous educational enterprise known as 'training in art appreciation'. It is something that modern pacifists have decided that *The Charge of the Light Brigade* and *The Death of Nelson* are not the ideal pictures for schools: but no more — for the quick extravert — are photographs of the Parthenon; or — for the quick introvert — reproductions of Raphael's Madonnas; or — for the slow introvert — some gay modernistic print from Germany.[1] Children need the opportunity of seeing many sorts of art and of picking and choosing what seems good to them. They may be taught to look at works of art from the historical or technical point of view, but they should not be taught to admire what their teacher considers admirable.

Roger Fry defined Taste as 'the negative avoidance of all that is ill considered or discordant', and in this sense the growth of Taste can be encouraged. I would define it more positively as the recognition of fine quality; and this too can be cultivated. The discordance to be avoided, however, is that between the child's own temperament and the work of art, not that between the work of art and the teacher's canon of beauty; the recognition of quality is to be sought in those things which a man himself finds beautiful, not in those which contemporary fashion alone prescribes. The man who says, 'I know

---

[1] Fortunately, in their own homes there is a reasonable chance of the children's having inherited the temperament of the parent who chose the pictures.

nothing about art but I know what I like', is not ridiculous; if his knowledge of his own taste is precise and sincere and his liking spontaneous his position is unassailable.

Not for a moment would I deny that there is Art which is great and art which is not. But, to quote Epictetus,[1] a thing is described as beautiful when it is 'most excellent according to its proper nature ... As the nature of each is different, each seems beautiful in a different way.' And as the nature of the man who sees it is different, so he sees different things to be beautiful. Some harmony between the artist's temperament and intellect, his conception and his medium, can create a work of art that may not give the highest degree of individual pleasure to every mind that contemplates it, but that yet has qualities of spiritual integrity that even minds uncongenial with its creator's can recognize. It is this recognition of something fine enough and strong enough in its kind to give the authentic thrill to the congenial temperament which it is the aim and prerogative of the trained student of art to achieve.[2] Yet this recognition of artistic validity for another type can never have the same assurance or give the same delight as the aesthetic contemplation of a work of art with which the observer himself is in harmony.

This examination, brief though it is, seems to show a peculiar quality in the relation between the men of different temperaments and the art they find beautiful, and between working artists and the art they produce. The introverts have a simple connection. The quick introvert's combination of formal relation and natural

---

[1] ARRIAN, *Discourses of Epictetus*, 3rd book, quoted Knight I, p. 41.

[2] HERBERT READ, *The Meaning of Art*, 1931, p. 3: 'the test of a serious student of art is that, whatever his own sense of beauty, he is willing to admit into the realm of art the genuine manifestations of that sense in other people at other periods'.

beauty is an immediate consequence of his study of cause and effect in the natural world. For him art is an integral part of life: he feels no contradiction between it and mortality, no conflict between it and the natural world.

> Its loveliness increases; it will never
> Pass into nothingness; but still will keep
> A bower quiet for us, and a sleep
> Full of sweet dreams, and health and quiet breathing.
> Therefore, on every morrow, are we wreathing
> A flowery band to bind us to the earth. . .

The slow introvert's capacity for representing human dignity in compositions that depend on tonal relation for their effect is equally a carrying-over into art of his predilections in other fields. He feels, like Cézanne, that art is a harmony parallel with nature. He, too, can make it a part of life, and find its creation 'an acknowledgement of the beauty of the universe, a task light and easy to him who looks at the world in the spirit of love; further, it is a homage paid to the native and naked dignity of man, to the grand elementary principle of pleasure, by which he knows and feels and lives and breathes'.[1]

The extraverts, however, have a double relation to art. Like the introverts they have a direct relation; the quick extravert takes his social elegancies into visual art; the slow extravert takes his facts, in portraiture, topographical, courtly and illustrative art. But besides this they have a second relation, a relation of escape.[2] The quick extravert who cannot comprehend and will not accept the natural world finds escape in the ecstasy and unreality of visions. He agrees with Anatole France:[3]

---

[1] WORDSWORTH, Preface to the 2nd edition of the *Lyrical Ballads*.

[2] The literature and art of escape, in so far as they are indeed art, are a means of escape not *from* but *for* the natural bent; but much of what is called the literature and art of escape is enjoyed not for its aesthetic qualities but as mere distractions and pastimes involving no such experience as aesthetic emotion.

[3] *La vie en fleur.*

'J'aime la vérité. Je crois que l'humanité en a besoin; mais certes elle a bien plus grand besoin encore du mensonge qui la flatte, la console, lui donne des espérances infinies. Sans le mensonge, elle périrait de désespoir et d'ennui.' It is precisely this dualism which Worringer recognizes in German art of the Middle Ages: 'on the one hand, the most acute direct comprehension of actuality, on the other hand, a super-actual fantastic play of line, uncontrolled by any object, vitalized only by its own specific expression'.[1]

The slow extravert, who cannot otherwise get away from the manifold facts of the natural world, finds escape in the generalization and unreality of ideal art: a realm of shadows in which he can feel himself 'dead to real life, detached from the needs of natural being, delivered from the bonds in which our dependence on exterior things holds us, freed from all the reverses, all the miseries of the finite world'.[2]

I do not pretend to understand the esoteric language of Nietszche and Schopenhauer's philosophy, but their 'Apolline' and 'Dionysiac' would seem to designate the double aesthetic state of the extravert:[3] the one a state of contemplation that produces an art of phenomena, the other a state of frenzy that produces an art of revelation.

Thus it would seem that the aesthetic philosophy of the visual arts must take two categories into account: art as a direct expression of temperament, that is valid for both extravert and introvert; and art as an escape for the temperament, that is valid for the extravert alone.

The visual arts, however, are but one of the fields that aesthetic philosophy must cover. The arts of literature, of drama, of movement and of music must likewise be

[1] WORRINGER, *Form in Gothic*, trans. Read, 1927, p. 64.
[2] Hegel, *Philosophy of Art*.
[3] On this see JUNG, *Psychological Types*, trans. Baynes, 1926, p. 172.

H

explored; and it may be that the introvert's escape into a compensatory beauty will be found there, rather than in the arts of sculpture, painting, architecture and decoration that have been studied here. Yet my impression is that the quick introvert remains perfectly consistent in taste, and appreciates in music that formal rhythm which pleases him in landscape, in poetry that intellectualized naturalism that delights him in decoration; and that the slow introvert finds the same pleasure in the psychological biography as he does in the psychological portrait, and in the psychological novel as in a composition of tonal relations. It would seem that the ideational power of the introvert serves to integrate even his relation to works of art.

Here I leave the theme to the more expert investigations of the psychologists and the profounder speculations of the philosopher. But as one who can perceive beauty, even though I cannot create it, I would add that such a conception of the differences between men, and such an acceptance of the subjective nature of beauty, need involve no moral or emotional disintegration. Vialle has written:[1]

'L'une de nos grandes déceptions est de sentir parfois, à tort ou à raison, que la beauté n'a pas d'existence hors des âmes, que nous tirons de nous-même toute la substance de nos joies, et que l'enchantement esthétique ne nous met pas en communication avec un univers de choses adorables.' But if we cannot conceive of beauty wholly apart from and exterior to ourselves, we can experience it not only as an individual experience, but also as a shared experience, a *coenaesthesia*. Tolstoy's conception of the brotherhood of man never found truer expression than when he wrote:

[1] *Le désir du néant*, p. 91.

CONCLUSION

'The chief peculiarity of [the feeling produced by art] is that the receiver of a true artistic impression is so united to the artist that he feels as if the work were his own and not someone else's — as if what it expresses were just what he had long been wishing to express. A real work of art destroys, in the consciousness of the receiver, the separation between himself and the artist, nor that alone, but also between himself and all whose minds receive this work of art. In this freeing of our personality from its separation and isolation, in this uniting of it with others, lies the chief characteristic and the great attractive force of art. . .'[1]

---

[1] *What is Art?* trans. A. Maude, n.d. (1899), p. 153.

NOTES TO THE ILLUSTRATIONS

THE plates have been chosen as typical examples out of many, any of which might have served to illustrate the same point. For this reason they have been treated as subordinate to the text, which only refers to them incidentally; but it seems advisable to give a few notes to indicate the reasons for which they have been chosen and the points which they illustrate.

Plates 1-4

These *Annunciations* have been grouped together because they illustrate the different treatment of the same scene by artists of varying temperament. The first, by Simone Martini,[1] illustrates the 'immobilized' or static scheme of the quick introvert artist. Neither Angel nor Virgin moves; the angel's drapery still floats from past movement, but the force of the wings seems in no wise to lessen the figure's human weight. The composition is strongly decorative in general line, and reveals the artist's delight in decorative details in the inlaid throne, the embroidered hems and delicate brocades of the dresses, the many-sided metal pot, and the feathers of the angel's wings, as well as in the lilies and the olive branch. The dramatic urgency of the scene is conveyed in two ways: by the constrained attitude of the Virgin, and by the oblique line of the angelic salutation that runs in beautiful Lombardic capitals from the angel's mouth to the Virgin's head. This inscription is in gold like the background, but its oblique line gives it the force of seen breath.

The second *Annunciation*, by Rubens, illustrates the dynamic scheme of the slow extravert. Nothing in it is in repose. The angel's hair still flutters from the descent; his foot is still strained with the effort of holding the ground. The Virgin's recoil is not spiritual, as in the former picture, but physical. Cherubs and slanting rays of light add movement to the scene just as Simone Martini's flowers add stillness.

[1] See p. 87.

NOTES TO THE ILLUSTRATIONS

The third *Annunciation*, by Botticelli,[1] illustrates the instability of the quick extravert scheme. Curiously enough this instability is less evident in the winged angel than in the Virgin: the angel's impetus drives her before him, and she must quickly fall.

The fourth *Annunciation*, by Domenico Veneziano, illustrates the typical composition of the slow introvert. An extreme calm pervades the scene; there is no indication that the angel has flown through the air, nor that the Virgin has been disturbed at her devotions by the news he brings. The little court closes the scene with a wall exactly parallel with the plane of the picture; and the garden gate seen through the archway reiterate the same plane.

Plates 5-8

This series similarly illustrates differences of composition in four pictures of seated Virgins.

In the first, Michelangelo's *Holy Family*, a subject that has necessarily a static quality, is infused with dynamic strength. The Virgin sits upon the ground, and turns back, one arm on the knee of Joseph who half sits behind her, to take the Child. The composition is instinctively thought of 'in the round': not even the emphasis on Joseph's silhouette can quite transmute it from sculpture into painting. The interest is concentrated into a sculptural group, linked by the play of muscle in body and limb.

The next picture, the *Coronation of the Virgin* by Velasquez, is not perhaps one of the most characteristic of his paintings; the critic is conscious that the subject has been imposed rather than chosen. Had it been possible, I had rather have illustrated the *Virgin Enthroned* by Hugo Van der Goes.[2] But even the Velasquez illustrates a frontality of composition and an absence of dramatic movement that is characteristic of the slow introvert painter, though the traditional cherubs do something to diminish the calm reasonableness of the whole.

[1] See p. 74.
[2] Heughel collection, Paris. Photograph in the Witt Library.

The third is the *Virgin Enthroned* of the Maître de Moulins:[1] a picture notable for the hieratic calm of its composition and the extreme beauty of its colour. The angels float and fly, but there seems nothing supernatural about their posture. The whole composition has the same spiritual quality as some Chinese painting of Buddha and his attendants.

The fourth of the series, an Assumption of the Virgin by El Greco, shows an 'ecstatic' scheme here employed for an appropriate subject. The Virgin both floats and ascends; the whole picture has an upward movement. Angels and cherubs have never seen this earth nor obeyed its law of gravity; they live free in light and cloud, and may become light and cloud at will. The whole scheme is supernatural; the only links with earth are the two saints below, and even they see visions and dream dreams.

Plates 9-12

This series of portraits cannot be said to illustrate great differences in composition, since the tradition of portrait painting is too strong and too reasonable to allow much scope for variation. They do, however, illustrate certain differences of feeling.

The hardest to choose was the first, the example of a portrait by a slow extravert. For the *genre* is that in which an artist of this temperament generally excels, and instead of illustrating one I should like to have illustrated a series, by Titian, Rembrandt, Rubens and Goya, to show the essential resemblance.

The slow extravert always sees his subject as a personage in a drama; the slow introvert sees him as a psychological study in repose. Again choice was difficult, for there was all Dürer and Holbein to choose from; but the Van Eyck chosen sufficiently illustrates the simplicity of composition, the minute and unconventional characterization, and the psychological insight that may be expected in a fine portrait by an artist of this temperament.

The third portrait — Gainsborough's charming picture of his

[1] See p. 83.

young daughters — is chosen to represent the quick extravert's love of a composition of quick and unfinished movement. Contrast it with Bartolommeo Veneto's static and decorative composition; and notice his characteristic enjoyment of the ornamental details in dress and jewels.

Plates 13 and 14

These two pictures are set here in contrast. Both are official portraits of Kings of Spain by Spanish artists, and both standing compositions. They illustrate the fact that subject and form do less than temperament to determine the ἦθος of a picture.

Plates 15-18

This series of landscapes, all with water in the foreground and hills behind, has been chosen to show that the main types of composition recur in landscapes.

The Cézanne shows, like almost all his landscapes, a horizontal line cutting across the composition. This is the landscape equivalent of the wall, parallel with the plane of the picture, that is generally found in other slow introvert compositions, and in the same fashion it gives the impression of a closed space.

The Patinir has been chosen to illustrate the element of fantasy and unreality that the quick extravert artist can find in nature. This seems no ordinary river, but the scene of some fairy tale in which nature's writ no longer runs.

The Cotman has been more fully treated in the text (p. 88). Its calm immobility affords a striking contrast to the fourth landscape, Constable's *Weymouth Bay*, in which wind and wave and cloud combine to give an impression of dynamic force and movement.

Plates 19-22

Four still-lifes have been chosen; as with portraits, the *genre* is strongly influenced by tradition. The first, by Goya, is a rather repulsive picture. Since he could not, in the *genre*, represent a living bird, he has portrayed one that is most unpleasantly dead. It cannot be taken as a typical slow extravert still-life, for

Goya was a pathological case; but it illustrates a personal interpretation of the *genre*.

The Caravaggio is interesting because it illustrates the slow introvert's tendency to emphasize the plane of the background. Exactly the same tendency is observable in the still-lifes of Cézanne.

The Chardin is the most typical still-life of all, for a still-life is a kind of picture that is congenial to the quick introvert artist. His enjoyment of texture and colour and quality there finds a simple and natural expression; and it is this perfectly spontaneous enjoyment which gives the quick introvert's still-lifes their essential value.

The fourth picture, Van Gogh's *Pommes de Terre*, illustrates the quick extravert's use of an unusual angle of vision to give novelty to his compositions.

Plates 23-36

Four examples of sculpture are here set together. The first, Bernini's *Saint Theresa*, illustrates the peculiar urgency of line which is characteristic of quick extravert sculpture. Further, it shows that a man of this temperament with sufficient technical mastery may even attempt a typically pictorial composition in stone.

The second — the statuette of the Countess of Holland — I have included because it seemed to be a sculptural expression of the same qualities as may be seen in such slow introvert portraits as Plate 10. I found it hard to discover; and it may perhaps serve to illustrate the fact that sculpture is not usually found to be a congenial medium by the slow introvert artist.

The third and fourth statues form a remarkable comparison. Maillol was Rodin's pupil; his *Pensée* is evidently related in subject to his master's *Penseur*; and yet there is a real contrast between the immobilized inertia of the one and the tense muscular effort of the other, that is perfectly characteristic of the contrast between the static composition of the quick introvert and the dynamic composition of the slow extravert.

Plates 27-30

The four pictures in this series are chosen to exemplify a characteristic *genre* for each type; the psychological study of an abnormal type, for the slow introvert; the *Fête Galante* for the quick extravert; the decorative relief for the quick introvert; and the satiric picture — Hogarth's *Bench* — for the slow extravert. With the latter has been set Goya's *Witches' Sabbat*, to show how the satiric *genre* may pass over into pure horror as the artist passes from sanity into an unbalanced state.

Plates 31 and 32

Two pictures chosen for contrast: the one a dynamic composition by Rubens, the other a quiet study of tonal relations by Dumesnil de la Tour.[1]

Plates 33-36

Four examples of decoration based on natural forms. The first and second show, I think, the difference between a quick introvert's and a quick extravert's adaptation of such forms; the element of strangeness in the second is comparable with Patinir's landscape. (Plate 16)

The second pair show that technical difficulties do not necessarily dictate the manner in which such forms are adapted. The wrought-iron gate, in spite of its material, has all the ease and sweetness of line which is denied the silk brocade, a material in which such curves find their easiest expression.

Plates 37 and 38

Two designs chosen because they show typical schemes; the first a composition that is unconsciously a contradiction of the law of gravity and the second deliberately intended to be dynamic.[2]

Plates 39-44

Plate 39 is intended to show that the slow extravert tendency towards rectilinear simplicity, broken only by a

[1] See p. 105.   [2] See p. 102.

multitude of identical structural units, finds expression in both classical and medieval architecture. To the two examples illustrated might have been added a block of modern flats. The next illustration portrays, in contrast, a building in which structure is obscured by much rich and irrelevant detail.

The next four illustrations are intended to show the strong difference of taste that may be expressed within the limits of the same architectural style. In the first pair Gothic architecture provides the contrast, in one case with the emphasis all on straight lines, in the other all on rounded curves; in the second two façades are illustrated, erected in the same town in the same century for churches of the same cult, and based on a similar scheme of columniation. The liking expressed in one for straight lines and classical simplicity is contrasted in the other by an enjoyment of mouldings, ornament and elaboration that gives a completely different effect to the whole. Incidentally these two façades show that the slow extravert is apt to be a better exponent of a strictly classical style than is the quick introvert.

Plates 45-48

This series of four plates attempts to illustrate the characteristics of rooms decorated by men of different temperaments. The Library of Sans Souci, in spite of its learned destination, is a room of infinite liveliness. Little in its decoration is symmetrical, nothing serious. Its ornament makes no pretensions to reasonableness, but succeeds in creating a whole of no little charm. In contrast to it Sir John Soane's parlour is reasonable to the point of dullness. Everything is symmetrical; much is straight. It has a characteristic massive dignity that is as near to pomposity as Sans Souci is to frivolousness.

The room at Chatsworth illustrated in the next plate is as dignified and much more splendid, but in a completely different mode. Everything that can be decorated is decorated, and decorated with an assurance and richness that shows a designer's faith in his own taste. With it may be contrasted the room shown in the last plate as St. Jerome's study: a room that some would prefer to any of the others, that may represent a real, idealized, or ideal workroom for Dürer himself. Nothing in it is deliberately designed to be decorative; the only useless object is a dried gourd that hangs from the ceiling; yet simplicity and appropriateness do in fact make it an artistic whole.

INDEX

INDEX

Delacroix, F. V. E., 27 n.2, 63, 70
    n.1, 93-5
Donatello, 81
Dresser, C., 102
Dumesnil de la Tour, 105, 122
Dupré, Prof., 23
Dura-Europos, frescoes from, 74
Dürer, Albrecht, 58, 106, 107, 119,
    124
Dynamic composition, 59, 61, 90-3
'Dynamic symmetry', 53 n.2

EASEL-PICTURES, 40
Economics applied to art, 54
Education in art, 109, 110
Egyptian art, 62, 67, 97
Einfuhlung, see Empathy.
El Greco, 73, 75, 77, 119
Ely, Lady Chapel, 82
Empathy, 57, 58 n.1, 59-61, 90
Empedocles, 19
English art, 65, 69
Environment, influence of, 66
Epictetus, 111
Epstein, Jacob, 27
Escape, art of, 112-14
Escorial, 68, 101
Exeter Cathedral, 82
Extravert, definition of, 23-5, 30
    —— quick, 34-6, 45-7, 65, 72-80,
    107, 112, 113
    —— slow, 31-4, 50-63, 65, 67, 89-102,
    107, 112, 113

FECHNER, G. T., 52, 53
Fergusson, James, 54
Ficino, Marsilio, 46, 47
Fine Arts, 45-65
Fitness for purpose, 53, 54
Flaubert, Gustave, 99
Flaxman, John, 94
Flemish art, 66
Florence, Medici Chapel, 101
    —— Pitti Palace, 101
Fontenay, Abbey of, 67
Fouillée, A., 21 n.6
Fountains Abbey, 67
Fourier, J. B. J., 22
France, Anatole, 112, 113
Francis, St., 43
French art, 48, 69, 71
Freud, Dr. Sigmund, 28
Frith, W. P., 98
Froment, Nicholas, 70 n.3
Fromentin, E., 90, 95

Frontal composition, 103
Fry, Roger, 27, 85, 93, 110
Furness Abbey, 67
Fuseli, Henry, 89

GAINSBOROUGH, THOMAS, 71, 73,
    75 n.3, 83, 119
Galen, 19, 21
Garrod, Prof. H. W., 64
Gaudi, 79
Genres, choice of, 71
German art, 48, 77, 113
Ghirlandajo, Domenico, 87
Gilbert, Sir Alfred, 77
Gill, Eric, 17 n.1
Gloucester Cathedral, Cloister, 82
Gnostics, 20
'Golden Section', 53
Goya, 64, 96, 97, 119-22
Granada, Alhambra, 82
    —— Cartuja, 81
Greek art, 27
Gregory Nazianzen, St., 51
Greuze, Jean Baptiste, 74
Grünewald, Matthias, 96
Guyau, 54 n.1
Guys, Constantin, 27 n.2

HALLER, A. VON, 21
Hals, Franz, 90, 98
Hambidge, Jay, 53 n.2
Hamilton, Lady, 73
Hazlitt, William, 38
Henry VIII, 69
Hippocrates, 19
Hirn, Prof. Yrjö, 17
Historical pictures, 56
Hogarth, William, 37, 40, 52, 90, 98,
    122
Holbein, Hans, 65, 69, 119
Holmes, C. J., 88
Home of Kames, Henry, 53 n.2
Hoogh, Pieter de, 106
Hooker, Richard, 38
Hugh of St. Victor, 41
Hulme, T. E., 27
Hume, David, 17 n.1, 20, 53, 109, 110
Hypnosis, 46

IMITATION in decoration, 102
Ingres, J. A. D., 64, 70 n.1, 94
Introvert, definition of, 23-5, 30, 36
    —— quick, 37-41, 47-50, 65, 80-9,
    107, 111, 112
    —— slow, 41-3, 63-5, 102-7, 112

INDEX

1. THE ANNUNCIATION, *by Simone Martini.* Quick Introvert

2. THE ANNUNCIATION, *by Rubens*. Slow Extravert

3. THE ANNUNCIATION, *by Botticelli.* Quick Extravert

4. THE ANNUNCIATION, *by Domenico Veneziano.* Slow Introvert

6. CORONATION OF THE VIRGIN, *by Velasquez.*

5. THE HOLY FAMILY, *by Michelangelo.*
Slow Extravert

8. ASSUMPTION OF THE VIRGIN,
    by El Greco. Quick Extravert

7. THE VIRGIN ENTHRONED, *by the Maître de Moulins.*
    Quick Introvert

10. PORTRAIT OF A YOUNG MAN,
by Van Eyck. Slow Introvert

9. PORTRAIT OF DOÑA ISABEL COBOS DE
PORCEL, *by Goya.* Slow Extravert

11. PORTRAIT OF THE ARTIST'S DAUGHTERS
by *Gainsborough.* Quick Extravert

12. PORTRAIT OF A MAN, *by Bartolommeo Veneto,*
Quick Introvert

13. PORTRAIT OF PHILIP IV, *by Velasquez.*
Slow Introvert

14.   PORTRAIT OF FERNANDO VII, *by Goya*.
Slow Extravert

15. L'ESTAQUE, *by Cezanne*. Slow Introvert

16. RIVER SCENE, *by Patinir*. Quick Extravert

17. **GRETA BRIDGE,** *by Cotman.* Quick Introvert

18. **WEYMOUTH BAY,** *by Constable.* Slow Extravert

19.   STILL LIFE, *by Goya.*   Slow Extravert

20.   STILL LIFE, *by Chardin.*   Quick Introvert

21.   STILL LIFE, *by Caravaggio*. Slow Introvert

22.   *LES POMMES DE TERRE, by Van Gogh*. Quick Extravert

24. THE COUNTESS OF HOLLAND,
by *Jacques de Gérine.* Slow Introvert

23. ST. THERESA, by *Bernini.* Quick Extravert

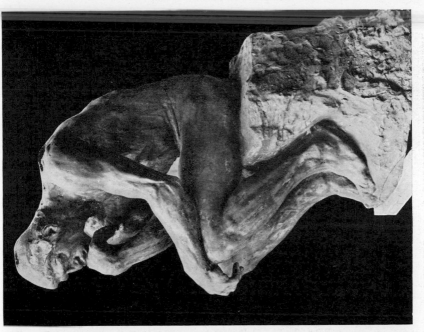

26. *LE PENSEUR, by Rodin.*   Slow Extravert

25. *LA PENSÉE, by Maillol.*   Quick Introvert

28. *CONVERSATION GALANTE, by Nicholas Lancret.*
Quick Extravert

27. THE FOOL CALABACILLAS, *by Velasquez.*
Slow Introvert

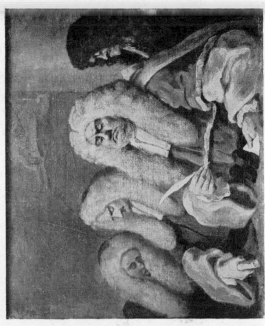

30. *a.* THE WITCHES SABBAT, *by Goya*
    b. THE BENCH, *by Hogarth.* Slow Extraverts

29. DETAIL OF THE LUDOVISI THRONE.
     Quick Introvert

31. CASTOR AND POLLUX, *by Rubens*.   Slow Extravert

32. *LE NOUVEAU NÉ, by Dumesnil de la Tour*.   Slow Introvert

33. FRIEZE FROM THE WEST DOOR,
NOTRE DAME DE PARIS.

Quick Introvert

34. CORSAGE ORNAMENT,
by René Lalique.

Quick Extravert

36. GATE OF WROUGHT IRON, CASA DE PILATOS.

35. SILK BROCADE, *French c. 1800.*

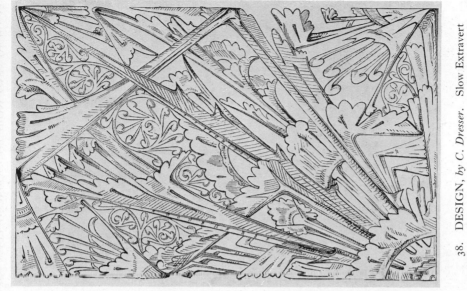

38.　DESIGN, *by C. Dresser.*　Slow Extravert

37.　DESIGN FOR A TEXTILE, *by Jean Pillement.*
Quick Extravert

39. *a*. THE PANTHEON OF AGRIPPA, ROME
     b. THE NOVICES' DORTER, POBLET.
           Slow Extraverts

40.   THE CLOISTER OF THE HIERONYMITES,
    LISBON.   Quick Extravert

41. THE TOWER OF ST. MARTIN, CLAMECY.
Slow Extravert

42.   EXETER CATHEDRAL: THE NAVE.
Quick Introvert

43. THE CHURCH OF ST. PIERRE, NEVERS
Slow Extravert

44. THE CHAPEL OF THE VISITATION,
NEVERS. Quick Introvert

45. THE LIBRARY, SCHLOSS SANS-SOUCI,
POTSDAM.   Quick Extravert

46.   THE FRONT PARLOUR, PITZHANGER MANOR.
Slow Extravert

47. THE STATE BEDROOM, CHATSWORTH.
Quick Introvert

48.   ST. JEROME IN HIS STUDY, *by Albert Dürer.*
Slow Introvert